CONTENTS

Editor: Robert Kershaw
Senior editor, specials: Roger Mortimer
Email: roger.mortimer@keypublishing.com
Design and mapping: Tim Mitchell Design
Advertising Sales Manager: Brodie Baxter
Email: brodie.baxter@keypublishing.com
Tel: 01780 755131
Advertising Production: Debi McGowan
Email: debi.mcgowan@keypublishing.com

SUBSCRIPTION/MAIL ORDER
Key Publishing Ltd, PO Box 300, Stamford, Lincs, PE9 1NA
Tel: 01780 480404
Subscriptions email: subs@keypublishing.com
Mail Order email: orders@keypublishing.com
Website: www.keypublishing.com/shop

PUBLISHING
Group CEO: Adrian Cox
Publisher, Books and Bookazines: Jonathan Jackson
Published by Key Publishing Ltd, PO Box 100, Stamford, Lincs, PE9 1XQ
Tel: 01780 755131 **Website:** www.keypublishing.com

PRINTING
Precision Colour Printing Ltd, Haldane,
Halesfield 1, Telford, Shropshire. TF7 4QQ

DISTRIBUTION
Seymour Distribution Ltd, 2 Poultry Avenue, London, EC1A 9PU
Enquiries Line: 02074 294000.

ISBN: 978 1 80282 657 9

We are unable to guarantee the bonafides of any of our advertisers. Readers are strongly recommended to take their own precautions before parting with any information or item of value, including, but not limited to money, manuscripts, photographs, or personal information in response to any advertisements within this publication.

BATTLES THAT CHANGED THE WORLD

Battles that Changed the World is a very special publication about decisive battles that altered the course of history. Our focus is on **Hastings 1066, Waterloo in 1815 and Stalingrad 1942-3.** All three engagements had a profound effect on the combatants and their histories.

The Battle of Hastings is a watershed being the last time a foreign invader has successfully seized and held the British Isles. Since 1066 no foreign power has successfully crossed the English Channel or North Sea, although the Spanish Armada in 1588, Napoleon in 1803-5 and Hitler's Wehrmacht in 1940 all tried. Defeat at Hastings resulted in 4,000 Saxon Thegns, the traditional English nobility, losing their ownership of land overnight to 200 Norman barons. It was a defining moment in British history. Afterwards England had a new language, laws, church, aristocracy and a new system of government enabling 10,000 Normans to hold 1 million Saxons in thrall.

Waterloo in 1815 is another battle defining the future history of Europe and was to herald the future development of the British Empire. It ended 23 years of unbroken French Revolutionary and Napoleonic wars and ushered in a period of general peace and prosperity, which with few exceptions was to last until 1914. The political map of Europe was redrawn in a form that would be recognizable to contemporaries today. Waterloo was the last mass battle of the 19th Century pre-industrial age to be fought in Europe over such a small physical area. Conflict was never again to be conducted in such splendid uniforms. The next major war would be fought in drab grey and khaki from the trenches of the First World War.

Hitler's defeat with the capitulation of the Sixth Army at Stalingrad in February 1943 was one of the turning points of the Second World War. It shattered the ascendancy of Wehrmacht Blitzkrieg established in 1939-40. Turkey was deterred from joining her traditional German ally while Hungary, Romania and Italy, who all lost sizable contingents during the battle were dismayed and encouraged to seek a way out of the war. Russia and the Allies realised for the first time that they would win. As with the previous two examples, the outcome of this one battle was world changing.

Each battle is introduced by an outline of the war from which it has been taken, with a short narrative of the course of the battle itself. The main commanders are reviewed, as are the typical experiences of the combatants, dwelling on the human aspect. Who were these men, what did they hear, see and feel?

Battlefield Detective articles expose the latest scientific or archaeological findings, debunk myths and offer investigative analysis of what really happened.

The Battlefield Tour reviews each battle from a 'Then and Now' perspective. Positions or viewing stands are picked out to best illustrate what occurred. Waterloo is the main battle portrayed and is shown through the exciting medium of specially commissioned three-dimensional scenes, showing what the combatants would have seen by the clock at different stages of the battle. Narrative eye-witness accounts illustrate each stand, relating what the participants saw at that particular point.

Each battle is rounded off with the Hollywood perspective of these momentous struggles. Popular feature films that portrayed the battles are reviewed and assessed for historical accuracy, authenticity and of course entertainment value!

This pseudo battlefield tour approach is aimed to appeal as much to the browser as those equally attracted to a historical novel or epic film. You don't have to be an expert to enjoy the tour!

Robert Kershaw

The Content structure for all three battles is:

Conflict introduction and battle narratives with maps and three-dimensional or top-relief battle diagrams.

A portrait of the commanders, soldiers and combatants: how they lived in the field, everyday activities, core beliefs, battle experiences and posing the question: what was it actually like?

Battlefield Stands provide a War Correspondent view of the battle, with maps to assist and point out where to go.

A 'battlefield detective' element examining myths, recent finds and unusual facts.

History according to the Movies reviews how accurate popular film portrayals have been.

King Edward the Confessor, a pious man, died childless on 5th January 1066. With no immediate heir, Harold Godwinson the Earl of Wessex had himself crowned King of England the following day. He was the foremost of a number of powerful earls. The Godwinson family owned land stretching from Cornwall to Kent in the south and East Anglia and part of the Midlands. Harold, who commanded the royal army, was immediately accepted as king by the Witanagemot, the Anglo-Saxon council of magnates. This was more a recognition of his military status than bloodline.

Harald Hardrada the king of Norway was a kinsman of the Canute family and had a distant claim to the English throne, which he decided to pursue. He began to prepare a Viking invasion of England in league with Harold's disaffected brother Tostig, previously the Earl of Northumbria. Duke William of Normandy had extracted a vague oath of allegiance from Harold in 1064 following a shipwreck and enforced stay in Normandy. He was similarly a blood heir and had been promised the succession in 1051 by Edward. Norman influence at the Confessor's court was, however, out manoeuvred by the rich and powerful Godwinson's family, to which Harold belonged. William was outraged when he was not chosen and likewise prepared for invasion.

In 1066, saints relics and the oaths sworn over them really mattered. William summoned his vassals, formed a coalition with Brittany, Flanders and the French and gathered troops. Emissaries were despatched to Pope Alexander in Rome to elicit his support. With God on his side William could offer plunder and influence in a subjugated England while guaranteeing a place in Heaven for all that fell in battle. Even nature was allegedly disturbed by Harold's

INVASIONS

wickedness. Halley's Comet, 'the terror of kings' and a sinister portent of change appeared in the April skies over England. Harold was dismayed.

William gathered a vast army of about 8,000 troops at Dives-sur-Mer in the Seine Estuary. A fleet of 700 ships was assembled to transport his multi-ethnic invasion force of Normans, Bretons, Flemings and French with their war horses across the Channel. It was the largest amphibious operation to be mounted since Roman times. Up to 14,000 men it is assessed would have been needed in and around the muster area to support and conduct such an enterprise. They waited for much of the summer months for favourable southern winds that never came.

Harold assembled his forces and fleet on the home side of the Channel in anticipation of the Norman invasion, considered to be the immediate threat. The core of his army was an elite bodyguard of Housecarls and Thegns, bulked out by the Fyrd, the levee raised by the Anglo-Saxon mobilisation system. These men were obliged to perform military duty for two months in exchange for holding five hides of land and served alongside every able-bodied Freeman called

An early English battle scene, reflecting the grisly reality of 11th Century combat at Stamford Bridge; the dead lie trampled under foot.

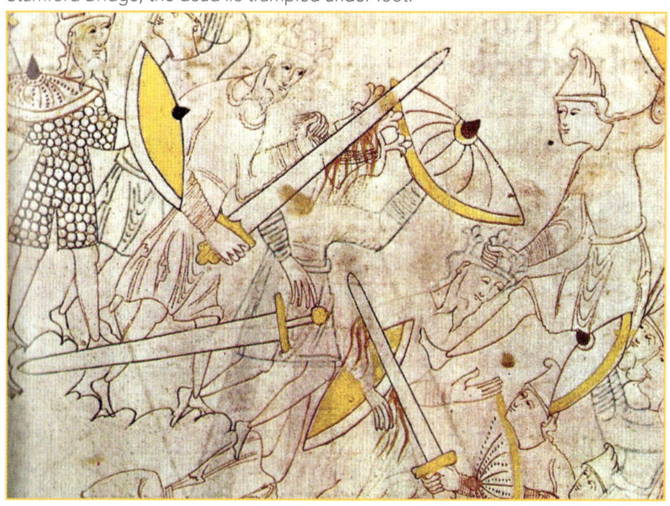

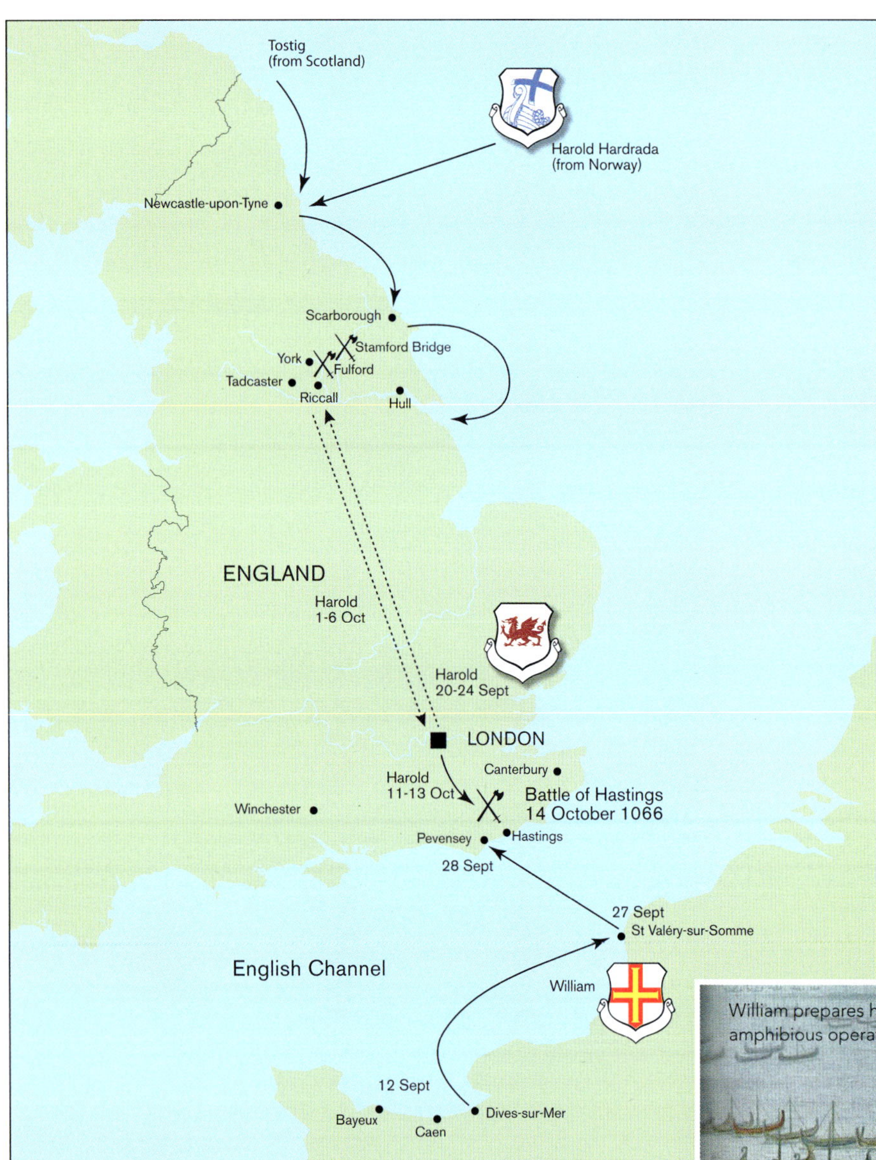

Harold was unexpectedly caught-out by the Viking invasion in the North by Harald Hardrada while waiting for the Norman invasion in the south. He was to fight two campaigns inside two weeks traversing the length of his kingdom twice.

process. Only 24 ships were left to ferry the battered Viking survivors back home after one of their worse reverses in England.

Two days after this momentous victory, William's fleet crossed the Channel in the south. They had moved from Dives to Saint-Valery at the mouth of the Somme River and the fleet picked up the needed southerly breeze, which took them to Pevensey Bay. Unexpectedly the landings were not contested. The Normans built a wooden castle on the site of an abandoned Roman fort and moved ten miles east to Hastings, where they established another firm base protected by a second prefabricated wooden castle.

Harold likely received the shocking news at York on 1st October and counter-marched to London in only five days to repel a second major invasion inside two weeks. He rode ahead with his Housecarls, having to leave his archers and the northern Fyrd behind. The southern Fyrd had to be regenerated yet again. Having disbanded it only a month before, Harold was testing the Anglo-Saxon mobilisation system to its absolute limit.

By the evening of 13th October, Harold was mustering his new force just outside the Anderswald Forest by the old hoar apple tree, a well-known landmark on Caldbec Hill seven miles north of Hastings. His core of Housecarls had marched 260 miles from York over a period of 12 days. The Normans

out to defend his shire. With the pressure of harvest time and no sign of the Norman ships and the onset of unpredictable autumn weather Harold ran out of time. On the 8th September he disbanded the Fyrd and returned to London.

Harald Hardrada unexpectedly struck first in the north, having crossed the North Sea in 300 longships. He joined Tostig with a smaller fleet in the Tyne and entered the Ouse River, raiding their way towards Riccal, ten miles from York. Harold's northern earls were defeated at the Fulford Gate just outside the city. Having just disbanded his southern Fyrd Harold abruptly marched 190 miles north in five days with his Housecarls to summon the northern levee. On the 25th September he completely surprised and destroyed the Viking army at Stamford Bridge, killing Hardrada and Tostig in the

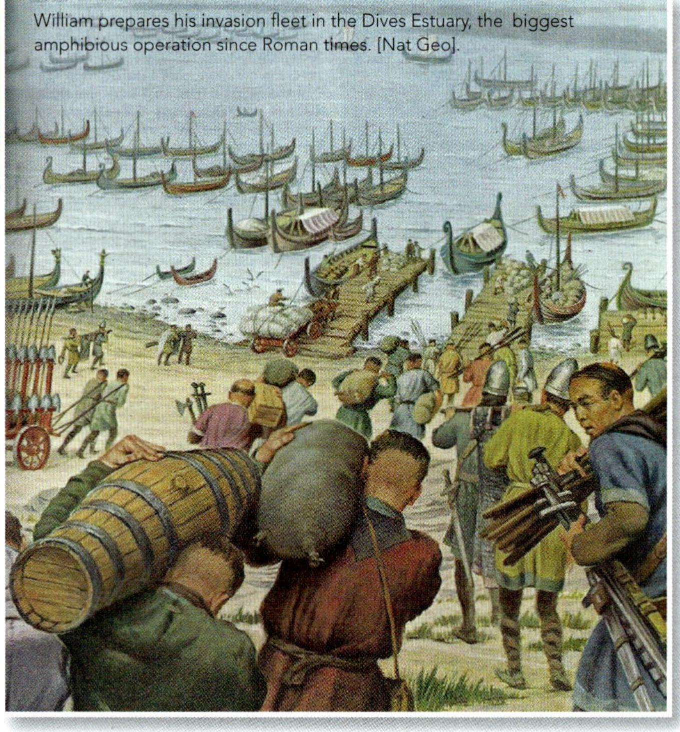

had been harrying the villages around Hastings and the English would have smelt the locally burning villages as they assembled during the evening before battle. William sought to bring the unseen English army to a quick decision in battle. Harold was striving to bottle the Normans up on the narrow causeway they had established for themselves surrounded by marsh and water around Hastings. He was astride the only route to London.

Harold was not ready. His precipitate 58 mile, three-day forced march from London was intended to surprise William, like the Vikings at Stamford Bridge. William was, however, too wily and Norman scouts detected the English approach. Both sides numbered between 7,000 to 8,000 men. Harold's force could well have been a half or a third bigger if he had paused. He was incensed at the ruthless Norman raiding, visited on his own property and people. After shattering the Vikings nearly three weeks before, he was convinced the Normans would follow suit.

Pevensey Castle today, now more than a mile from the 1066 coastline. The prefabricated wooden castle was replaced by the existing stone castle.

In 1066 this was a complex of marshy inlets and lagoons. This view clearly shows the original low lying land to the left of the pebble beach front.

The most decisive battle fought on English soil

THE BATTLE OF HASTINGS
13TH OCTOBER 1066

The Normans marched the six miles from their wooden castle at Hastings to the crest of Telham Hill in about one and a half hours. Forming up on Senlac Hill opposite was Harold's army, still pouring out of the forest to its rear. The weather on 14th October was unremarkable. There is no comment, a typical autumn day, not too hot and it did not rain. Harold's precipitate advance and readiness to confront the Normans before more resources could be mobilised was a departure from his previously considered forced march and surprise attack at Stamford Bridge. He was spiritually taken aback when he learned about William's Papal support and the threat of excommunication. William wore the holy relics, over which Harold had allegedly sworn, around his neck in battle. Some of the Fyrd were uncomfortable to realise that perhaps God was not on their side and may have deserted or delayed their arrival.

Despite all this, Harold's battle tactics were sound. His shield wall lay astride the road to London on a prominent crest-line on an isthmus surrounded my marsh. Much of William's armoured horse capability was negated at a stroke. Both flanks of the hill feature, where the present Battle Abbey now stands, were steep and covered by trees and undergrowth. The killing ground to its southern front varied in gradient from 1 in 15 near the present road to 1 in 33 at the western end of the ridge. Both sides faced unfamiliar tactical formations.

The static interlocking solidarity of Harold's shield wall exuded a physical and psychological menace that was unknown to William's men. They were more used to mobile raiding and static sieges in Normandy. Norman Chronicler William of Poitiers saw it as an innovation in warfare. *'Indeed this was a battle of a new type: one side vigorously defending attacking: the other resisting as if rooted to the ground'.*[1]

Harold's men warily regarded three unusual lines formed in three divisions before them: archers ahead of heavy infantry and stranger still, massed lines of cavalry behind them. It is believed William's

Fighting from the crest of Senlac Hill negated the impetus and height advantage of the Norman horsemen.

Harold lost two brothers at the height of the battle, a devastating personal and political loss. The loss of a war lord to whom his soldiers owed personal allegiance could unhinge an 11th Century battle.

army formed up with 1,500 archers, 4,000 heavy infantry and some 2,000 mounted knights. Harold's Housecarls and Thegns formed the front ranks of a shield wall, stretching 400 yards either side of his Wessex Dragon banner in the centre. His numbers were similar; three quarters of them were mustered Fyrd and freemen, the rest professional Housecarls and Thegns.

Although both sides were surprised when the other army came into sight, they essentially looked alike. The primary difference was that Harold had probably left his archers behind in the north. Only one English archer appears in the Bayeux Tapestry representation of the battle. Many of his front-line carried axes as well as swords and spears. Facing them were bowmen, heavily mailed infantry with sword, spear and shield and mounted knights with lance, sword, kite-shaped shields and heavy maces.

After much braying of trumpets, posturing and bellowing at each other the Norman infantry advanced up the steep hill at about nine or ten o'clock after volleys of arrows had swept the opposing line. The Norman tactics aimed to take out bite-size chunks of the shield wall and immediately exploit any breaches with conroys of heavy cavalry, groups of between 10 to 20 knights. The Norman infantry

'Assailed by volleys of spears, throwing axes and heavy stones attached to sticks'

were thinned as they climbed the slope assailed by volleys of spears, throwing axes and heavy stones attached to sticks hurled down from above. They made no indentation on the shield wall. That the Norman infantry did not excel is marked by their conspicuous mis-representation in the Bayeux Tapestry.

So aggressive was the English response to this initial assault that the Bretons, both on foot and horse to the left of the Norman line, recoiled and broke away. They began streaming down the hill. This mid morning development was the first crisis of the battle. It was rumoured that Duke William was down and he had to pull back his helmet to expose his face, and threaten his men with his lance to get them to reform. Part of the English shield wall may well have moved forward to exploit the retreat and the English were poised to fall upon the fragmenting Norman left wing. One or both of Harold's brothers were cut down at this point which caused the advance to falter even as William sought to retrieve the Norman situation. It was to prove the decisive point of the battle and a missed opportunity for Harold. Two brothers lost signalled the political demise of a powerful English dynasty, as well as dismaying their Housecarls and Fyrd. Overcome by blood lust the Fyrd continued on down the slope but were cut off by William's mounted knights, whom he had either rallied or reinforced. A segment of Harold's right was therefore sliced off and butchered piece-meal in front of the shield wall.

What Harold gained by his inspirational presence, bonding while fighting shoulder to shoulder at the shield wall, was lost in command mobility. William, on horseback was able to quickly traverse the depth and breadth of the battlefield to make his leadership count where it was needed. The English way of war appeared hidebound by tradition. They chose to fight dismounted, leaving their horses in the rear, whereas the armoured Norman knights were open to new and more versatile tactics. There was no immediate advantage, because both sides became locked in a bloody stalemate that lasted most of the day. Despite frequent pauses for breath, Norman attacks were unable to breach the shield wall.

Left: Harold fighting beneath his banner in this heroic representation of Hastings.

Bottom centre: A modern re-enactment demonstrating the limited room to fight at the shield wall

WAS THE ENGLISH SHIELD WALL BROKEN BY A SUCCESSION OF FEIGNED RETREATS?

Harold's death was the immediate cause of the English collapse but it is often argued the shield wall had already been fatally weakened by a succession of feigned retreats. Norman poet Robert Wace claimed the English:

'…Were deceived by the pretended flight, and great mischief thereby befell them; for if they had not moved from their position, it is not likely that they would have been conquered at all; but, like fools, they broke their lines and pursued'.[2]

The death of Harold's two brothers Leofwine (figure with axe) and Gyrth (standing to his right, being attacked by a horseman's lance) may have caused the English attack on the Bretons to falter. It is not known precisely, but their deaths were important enough to be represented in the Bayeux Tapestry.

According to the more reliable chronicler William of Poitiers this happened on three separate occasions, while William of Malmesbury cites it as the chief reason for the Norman victory. The Breton retreat back into the valley mid-morning was a near rout and hardly deliberate. Primitive arrangements for command and control would have made it near impossible to tell riders when, where and how far to retreat. It is suspected that Harold's failure to capitalise on this opportunity may have cost him the battle. The shield wall was not impervious to movement and could have been in the process of moving forward at this point. Possibly one or both of Harold's brothers: Gyrth and Leofwine, died during this follow-up, which would clearly have caused the advance to falter. William also feared dead, raised his helmet and exhorted his men to counter-attack and the over-exposed Fyrd was caught out in the open by cavalry and slaughtered. ➤

Despite the practical difficulty of executing sham flights there is evidence that the Normans used such a stratagem at Arques in 1053, at Messina in 1060 and later at Cassel in 1071. Such ruses were commonplace raiding tactics. Individual mounted detachments, conroys or their multiples could quite plausibly have briefly clashed riding along the shield wall and then broken off to draw the lesser disciplined Fyrd after them, down the slope in unwise pursuit. These would have been small scale actions. Only a quarter of Harold's force was made up of disciplined professionals. Stalemate at the shield wall would have encouraged the employment of all sorts of Norman tactical ruses at the flanks or weak points to hack away segments of the defence.

By late in the day English strength had been whittled down by a series of cumulative costly side-actions. A rain of arrows descended upon the weary survivors, perhaps a late re-supply. Coming in at high and direct angles, the exhausted English, less alert, found them difficult to avoid and they caused mayhem among the less protected Fyrd in depth who could see even less.

Once Harold's two brothers had fallen, the shock of Harold's wounding was terminal for the shield wall, which would have lost its best men by this stage of the battle. A whole variety of ruses and combat stratagems would have played a key part.

Even the Norman horsemen recoiled from the shield wall.

Norman Knights counter attack to catch the defenceless Saxon Fyrd in the open in a scene from Justin Hardy's film re-enactment 1066.[Channel 4].

The Saxons warily regarded disciplined lines of Norman infantry behind their archers with horsemen backing them up, an unprecedented formation. [Bibliothèque Nationale]

Not only were the Normans nonplussed by this impermeable wall of interlocking shields, both sides were also taken aback at the length of time this all-out fighting was taking, far beyond the normal fleeting clashes that characterised medieval warfare. Feigned retreats were employed to draw off the unstable Saxon Fyrd. The Normans had employed similar tactics at Arques in 1053 and at Messina in Sicily six years before. This was William's first set-piece battle in command. Harold had just won his last battle and instinctively appreciated he had to hold on until dusk and reinforcements. William normally cautious in risking all-out battle applied all his mounted skirmishing experience and guile through tactical ruses to whittle down the Saxon strength to the point where it would impact upon the integrity of the shield wall. Harold, having lost two brothers, was already politically mortally wounded.

Combined flat trajectory cross-bow fire with volleys of arrows arcing overhead rained down in depth on the less protected Fyrd, even as the Housecarls in the front rank raised shields to ward off direct attacks by knights jabbing with lance and sword. Harold possibly pierced by an arrow in the eye was overwhelmed by a group of Norman knights. Transfixed by a lance to the chest, he was beheaded, disembowelled and allegedly castrated in a frenzied assault. After Harold went down, the shield wall fragmented into a series of tight knots of resistance, where the surviving Housecarls, Thegns and remaining Fyrd fought viciously to the death. Others sought flight through the woods. The Normans received one bloody riposte at the Malfosse or 'evil ditch' to the north west of Senlac Hill, stumbling into a trap as they pursued their quarry into the gathering gloom. The battle was over. It is likely that half of Harold's force perished, twice as many as the 2,000 Norman dead.

Harold had fought this battle with his entire political leadership and the cream of his professional retainers. They were all now dead. Overnight the ownership of English land changed. Some 4,000 Saxon Thegns were to be replaced by 200 Norman Barons, one million Saxons would be ruled by 10,000 Normans. As one Norse poet was to lament:

'Cold heart and bloody hand,
Now rule the English Land…'[3]

'the cream of Harold's entire political leadership were all now dead'

After some initial skirmishing London submitted to William by the middle of November and he was crowned King of England on Christmas day 1066. The Battle of Hastings resulted in new laws, language, aristocracy, church and a new system of government. It was the last time the UK mainland was to be conquered and held by a foreign invader.

1. William of Poitiers, *The Deeds of William, Duke of the Normans and King of the English*, L Thorpe trans, The Bayeux Tapestry and the Norman Invasion, 1973, P. 51.
2. Wace, *Le roman de Rou*, 'The Romance of Rollo'.
3. R Holmes, *War Walks 2*, P. 14.

One loved, one respected,
both ruthless

HAROLD GODWINSON, KING OF ENGLAND

Harold Godwinson, King of England was about 45 years old at the battle of Hastings. He had been the king's right hand man when Edward the Confessor died in 1066, so it came as no surprise when the Anglo-Saxon Witan or council accepted his accession. The Godwinson clan had dominated royal circles for over a generation. Within eight months he was pitched into a crisis when two other contenders for the supremacy chose to invade, Harald Hardrada with a Viking army to the north and Duke William of Normandy to the south.

Harold was an imposing good-looking man with Norse features, charismatic, long-haired and moustached in the Saxon style. He arrived at the battlefield with a considerable military reputation for dash and quick decision. In 1062 he had defeated Edward the Confessor's Welsh enemies during a daring mid-winter assault. Three weeks before Hastings he had shattered Hardrada's Viking army near York, following an epic forced-march that caught the Norse army totally unprepared, before they could even don chain mail. Military profile rather than his nebulous family claim had secured his kingship on the death of the rather pious and monastic Edward earlier the same year.

Harold's attraction to the English was this military reputation, important in a fractured society during dangerous times. With it came genuine love and respect for his charismatic style of leadership. Unlike William of Normandy, much respected by his soldiers, Harold's generous and warm nature elicited affection and fierce loyalty. William had identified this during Harold's enforced stay in Normandy in 1064. Harold had rescued two of his men-at-arms trapped in quick-sands during a crossing of the River Couesnon near Saint- Michael on a military expedition. This made Harold popular with the Norman soldiers and William knighted him for it. He would doubtless have shrugged off the loss as the unavoidable consequence of active operations. Harold inspired fierce allegiance by leading from the front. His Housecarls marched an epic 190 miles to York, fought a major battle at Stamford Bridge and were back at Hastings in the south, another 260 miles, all conducted during three weeks of campaigning. Harold demonstrated physical endurance and decisive resolve, and took his men with him. He demonstrated energy and

Harold (left) and the Norman cropped William thoughtfully regard each other in this artist's impression of a scene during Harold's enforced stay in Normandy in 1064. [Nat Geo]

personal magnetism by quickly recruiting a Fyrd army in the middle of the northern crisis and then just as quickly resurrected the same southern Fyrd that had been disbanded, after waiting fruitlessly all summer for the Normans.

That Harold was a 'people' person was demonstrated by his uncharacteristic dash to Hastings to alleviate the suffering of his personal dependents, who were mercilessly harried by the Norman army. A whole swathe of villages at Hailsham, Herstmanceux, Ashburnham, Crowhurst, Filsham and Horstede were wasted by the Normans, losing half their taxable value between 1066 and the Domesday Book census of 1085. According to one story, Harold's faithful Reeve was slowly hanged from the gable of his own manor house at Crowhurst.[4] Harold was after revenge.

His rash actions prior to the battle were uncharacteristic. He ignored advice to pause for further reinforcements before grappling with William. Normally his predilection for quick and decisive action was tempered by practical experience. Harold like everyone else in medieval society was deeply religious. It is conceivable and evidence suggests that he was taken aback at William's Papal support, his possession of the holy relics over which he had allegedly sworn to uphold William's claim to the throne and the threat of excommunication. Such issues counted and were important and following the sinister appearance of Halley's Comet that spring, he felt spiritually unmanned. He sought immediate battle, trading surprise against expanding his own force by as much as half again. Relying on God's judgement, he left his archers in the north, unable to arrive in time.

During battle the Anglo-Saxon shield wall derived strength from Harold's leadership from the front. Stymied perhaps by an island imperviousness to new military ideas, William's armoured horsemen would carry the day, but only after a fiercely close-matched battle. Harold's static leadership may have cost him dear at the battle climax, when the Bretons retreated. William on horseback was able to move to the crisis point and inspire a counter-response. The extent to which Harold's personal military prowess was venerated by his own men is evidenced by their total collapse on his death. God, as the Norman chroniclers constantly remind us, clearly favoured William.

Harold was loved, whereas William was respected by his men. Harold typically rescued two of William's men from quick-sands during a military expedition during his stay in Normandy. William would have shrugged off their loss. [Bayeux Tapestry]

DUKE WILLIAM OF NORMANDY

William 'the Bastard' Duke of Normandy was about 38 years old at the battle of Hastings, five to seven years Harold's junior. He was of stocky build and Viking descent, clean-shaven with the characteristic half-cropped Norman hair at back and sides. His tough stout countenance would deteriorate to corpulence in later life. He fought the battle with the same mixture of guile and ruthless tenacity that had characterised his own childhood fight for survival. He had inherited his father's title from Duke Robert at the tender age of seven, the only, but illegitimate son. Factional in-fighting saw many of his protectors murdered before he had emerged and established himself in 1060. Almost all his young manhood was taken up in armed struggle against his own barons, neighbours and overlord, the King of France. At 30 years old he was proving to be the pre-eminent warrior ruler in northern France. Normandy was ruled with an iron fist.

William was the product of this violent background. He was brave, brutally ruthless and could be cruel. This was shown by his dispassionate treatment of the English dead after Hastings. When the besieged citizens of Alençon taunted his humble background by hanging cow hides from its walls in 1051 (his mother was the daughter of a tanner), he had some of its citizens skinned alive on capture. Naked ambition and a love of wealth led him to pursue the English claim, allegedly promised 15 years before by Edward the Confessor, a blood relative. Harold dubiously swore support over holy relics in 1064, so the outraged William sought Papal support for his cause. This was typical of his considered and deliberate diplomacy, when he decided after skilfully attracting Breton, Fleming and French support to his banner, to invade.

William was a methodical and focussed planner, an adept project manager in modern parlance. He was a serious, cautious and careful man, the antithesis of Harold, a man to be respected rather than revered. A powerful warlord, he commanded allegiance through success in battle, which provided tangible rewards for all that followed him. Uncharacteristically, he took two enormous risks: an amphibious invasion and acceptance of a set-piece battle in England. Both had no back-up in the event of failure. Sieges and mounted raids characterised Norman warfare, pitched battle was high risk. Nevertheless, William operated from a secure base in Normandy. The deaths of the King of France and Count of Anjou had removed all border threats, while his marriage alliance with Flanders and success in mobilising Papal support cleared the way for invasion.

This invasion was meticulously prepared and executed. Transporting an army of 7,000 with 2,000 warhorses across the channel in 700 open boats was no mean achievement. On arrival the Normans assembled pre-fabricated wooden castles at Pevensey and Hastings. From these secure bases the Normans wasted the surrounding countryside, securing supplies and goading Harold to reveal his army and attack. Unlike the arrogantly confident Vikings, the careful William had his scouts out when Harold approached. Nobody was going to surprise him in this strange land.

William used continental heavy infantry and cavalry tactics at Hastings, jointly operating with archers. The Saxon shield wall was as unfamiliar to the Normans as the set piece divisions of mutually supporting infantry and horse were to the Saxons. It was Williams's first set-piece battle in command. He approached it by applying the same mobile hard-hitting tactics his raiders would have applied in Normandy. It was a tortoise versus stoat confrontation.

The battle was won by intelligent leadership, personally directed from the front with a mixture of guile and brute force. The intrinsic worth of mounted knights against foot was lost on the slopes of Senlac Hill, the consequence of sound tactical decisions taken by Harold. William's methodical application of brute force rather than any innate technical or tactical superiority, was what won the day. Bite-size mutilation of the shield wall was the key to success, rather like hounds worrying at a stag. These were achieved by feigned retreats and sudden attacks at weak points. Any opportunity to catch the hapless Fyrd in the open was taken during a steady cumulative wearing down of resistance by piece-meal attacks. High arcing volleys of arrows combined with direct flat trajectory strikes with cross-bow quarrels were employed throughout.

William had fought for survival ever since childhood. Experience had taught him to methodically plan for all eventualities. He was quick-witted, fierce and cunning with such a resilient strength of purpose that convinced his followers that God was surely on their side.

William's distinctive half-cropped hair is apparent in this Bayeux Tapestry representation

4.   Reeve story, P. Marren, *1066*, P. 98.

Behind the Saxon Shield Wall

THE ENGLISH

Norman poet Robert Wace described what the Norman infantry would have seen as they toiled up the slopes of Senlac Hill to attack the shield wall at its crest:

'The English stood firm on foot in close ranks, and carried themselves right boldly. Each man had his hauberk on, with his sword girt, and his shield at his neck. Great hatchets were also slung at their necks, which they expected to strike heavy blows'.

The English regarded the wary Norman approach with mixed feelings. Many were arrogantly confident. Barely three weeks before they had decimated the Viking ranks at Stamford Bridge. Some of the Housecarls were still showing flesh wounds, battered and bruised from the fight. They were weary. Harold's core bodyguard had travelled 190 miles from London to York, fought a battle and rode 260 miles south again to Senlac Hill. Having fought one pitched battle and about to embark on another, they were physically and emotionally past their peak. Nevertheless, being at the top end of society, they had most to lose. The traditions espoused by the Anglo-Saxon vernacular poem *The Battle of Maldon* made much of the Housecarl's duty not to leave the field, even if his lord had fallen. Like the Thegns and other freemen warriors fighting for the earls, they were a unique and close knit warrior society and would fight to the death to repel the invader.

Standing behind them in the ranks, two to three men back, were three or four files of the Anglo-Saxon Fyrd. These were the men from the southern shires who had already been called out before in late June to oppose an invasion that never came. They were disbanded on the 8th September to gather a late harvest. By the end of the month they heard the king was battling the Vikings with the northern Fyrd, but there had been little time to reflect. Twenty days after they were stood down they were immersed in a rush of strange raiders whose hair was half cropped at the back and sides. Their women were raped, families butchered, houses set alight and their livestock killed. They were fearful yet burned with hatred, standing with their betters, pounding their swords rhythmically against their shields sustained by the bellowing chorus of *Uit! Uit* Out! Out! Robert Wace called them *'a great assemblage of villainaille, of men in everyday clothes'.* Many wore leather caps with a mix of old helmets, some with tough hide coats to offer some protection against sword cuts. This was an emergency, freemen had also been called up with the general Fyrd to protect their threatened shire.

The smell of burned villages was in the air. It added to a sense of unease. During the preceding spring a fiery comet had been seen streaking across the sky, night after night. What did it mean? The harbinger of doom or momentous change? Death and destruction had already come in its wake. The Normans had also unfurled a Papal banner. Relics and the bones of the Saints meant a lot to these simple folk. Was God with the Normans? Maybe so, but many abbots and deacons were also fighting beneath Harold's standard.

Wace captured the atmospheric tension permeating the English ranks as the Normans perceptibly increased their pace, closing the final few metres to the shield wall:

'The English were to be seen stirring to and fro, were going and coming; troops ranging themselves in order; some with their colour

Both sides looked alike, this Saxon Housecarl would have had a circular shield.

rising, others turning pale; some making ready their arms, others raising their shields; the brave man rousing himself to fight, the coward trembling at the approach of danger'.[5]

Both sides did not run at each other. Despite the storm of missiles exchanged between the shield wall and approaching mass, the men on foot were wary and looking for a potential opening on the opposite side. As they locked weapons and grappled the Normans recoiled from the shield wall. The professional English warriors at the front looked for exposed peripheries, and lopped them off with axe or sword. Only elite Housecarls wielded the two-handed Danish battle-axe. At four to five feet long, the lengthy haft gave range and power to the swing. The Normans quickly appreciated that such a weapon differentiated the quality warrior.

The Saxon Fyrd and Freemen were only lightly armed.

and jabbing lances and swords across the top of the shield wall. Horses might be felled by an axe or tripped by spear jabs, riders dragged off their horses and despatched by axe and sword or dragged inside to be dealt with by the Fyrd. Breaking ranks was fatal to the Saxon defender. When the Bretons broke on the Saxon right the Fyrd rushed after them and were cut down to a man by the Norman horse. Conroy raiding sweeps of groups of ten to twenty knights were irresistible in the open.

Medieval battles rarely lasted more than an hour or so. Too much was at risk in an era more used to the skirmish or quick raid to gamble all on a deliberate battle. Exhaustion and the deaths of key Saxon leaders took their toll. Harold had already lost two brothers, an irredeemable political and socio-economic loss, when he was allegedly hit in the eye by an arrow. Wace describes how *'in his agony he drew the arrow and threw it away, breaking it in his hands; and the pain to his head was so great that he leaned upon his shield'*. True or not, Harold was cut down and dismembered in a frenzied attack

Unable to penetrate, the Norman horsemen could only thrust at the Saxons across the top of the shield wall. [Channel 4].

He could just as easily hook the unwary from their feet or entangle a shield and brain the man with the iron-capped spike at the end as swiftly dismember him on reversing the blade when he was down. Small throwing axes were accurately hurled, spinning end over end into the enemy line at 50 yards. Their swift approach was difficult to discern amid the melee and almost impossible to parry.

The Saxon wall depended upon tight interlocking shields and emotional bonding for its integrity. Warriors had implicit trust that the man to his left would jab and thrust across his front to the right. Crashing up against it unbalanced Norman foot soldiers who became momentarily vulnerable to spear and sword jabs, coming over the top of the wall. Axe-men needed space, and would trade this in concert with an accompanying sword man. One step back created an enticing opening into which an unwary Norman might plunge only to be despatched by the backward swing of an axe or a vicious accompanying sword thrust. An accomplished axe-man could wield his finely balanced blade and haft in a two-handed figure of eight sequence for some time. Skilled warriors did not expend energy hacking and slashing, they employed economical pre-practiced fighting sequences, cannily deducing any weakness on the opposing side. Spearmen jabbed at face level, forcing their opponents to raise their shield which temporarily blind them to attack from another companion. Spear points jabbing in unison outside the shield wall were difficult to penetrate. The integrity of the shield wall was all-important. *'They were so densely massed'* described Norman Chronicler William of Poitiers *'that the men who were killed could hardly fall to the ground'*.[6]

The shield wall had never faced armoured horsemen before. Harold's astute hill crest siting did much to compensate for their weight and height advantage. Even so, the ground trembled as the great Norman Destriers rode up. To their surprise and consternation the Norman knights ricocheted off the pliable barrier. All they could do was ride alongside and try to barge an opening while defending

by a group of Northern knights. Whether William had received a re-supply of arrows is not known. The English had left their archers in the north. Tired and totally immersed in the melee of close combat it was difficult to hold a crumbling shield wall with missiles raining down in depth.

Even as the defeated English army was cut down straggling away from the field, chased by the merciless Norman horse, they retained their innate aggression. Housecarls fought on despite having lost their lords. As dusk fell pursuing Norman knights tumbled into an unseen ravine, the *Malfosse* or 'evil ditch'. Immediately the retreating Saxons rounded on them, slaughtering them in large numbers. The hard fought battle had been close-run. Defeat was, however, total. Saxon survivors would never again enjoy society as they knew it before 14th October 1066.

---

5. Wace, *Le roman de Rou*.

6. Poitiers, *The Deeds of William, Duke of the Normans and King of the English*.

Breaching the Shield Wall

A Norman knight. The raised pommel forward and rear increased stability in the saddle and the kite shaped shield gave added protection to his exposed legs. The Saxons were not familiar with fighting armoured horsemen.

THE NORMANS

Norman battle tactics were as unfamiliar to the English as their close-cropped appearance and language. Chronicler William of Malmsbury described the differences between the assailants on that 'fatal day'.

'The English at the time wore short garments, reaching to the mid knee; they had their hair cropped, their beards shaven, their arms laden with gold bracelets, their skin adorned with punctured designs; they were wont to eat until they became surfeited and to drink until they were sick'.

The Normans were arrayed in a strange battle formation. There were three divisions of three lines, with the Bretons to the left, Flemish and French on the right and William's men in the centre. Some 1,500 archers were positioned ahead of 4,000 heavy infantry with 2,000 knights waiting expectantly in the rear for the first signs of a breach in the shield wall. William of Malmsbury described the Normans as

'exceedingly particular in their dress' and *'fierce in attacking their enemies'*. Unlike the solid formation ahead of them, the Normans were *'ready to use guile or to corrupt by bribery'*. They were accessible to new ideas and fought as such, *'they weigh treason by its chance of success, and change their opinions for money'*. This was a clash of two cultures.[7]

William's men were independent-minded adventurers, like their Viking forefathers. They fought for plunder and economic gain as well as for their lords. Buoyed by Papal support and the promise of power and riches by Duke William all the soldiers had participated in a high-risk enterprise. By crossing the Channel, a perilous voyage in questionable weather, they had burned their boats. Going back was hardly an option. They were a disciplined force, as evidenced by William's masterful logistics and tight control. He mustered a force of 10,000 to 14,000 men and kept them intact and focussed throughout a long summer in the Dives and Somme estuaries prior to the crossing. The biggest and riskiest amphibious operation mounted since Roman times paid off, the landings were unexpectedly unopposed. William's landing force was an inter-ethnic mix of about 2,000 Bretons, 1,500 Flemings and French and 4,000 Normans. More diverse than the English, but unlike them, the majority were hardened professionals, mercenaries and accordingly equipped.

Two weeks of rapine and plunder in the surrounding English villages followed the months of enforced inactivity in France, a deliberate policy to goad Harold into battle. After the disciplined restrictions placed on their sojourn in the Dives estuary awaiting favourable winds, unrestricted warfare against defenceless civilians had been welcomed by warriors used to raiding back home, especially as it formed part of God's will. With so little opposition to date, William's men probably felt confident they would give the effeminate English a beating. They had not even appeared to defend the helpless villages they razed to the ground, and after this battle there would be even more.

Armoured horsemen had been gaining steadily in importance on the Continent but were less well known in England. Norman knights were identically armed and clad like the Housecarls and Thegns although knights wore knee-length mail hauberks, split front and rear for riding with an integral mail hood. Helmets could be hammered from a single piece of iron or made of riveted segments, padded within with leather or cloth to cushion the head against blows. These conical helmets often had a nasal guard to protect the nose and face, giving the wearer a grim impersonal appearance, which could be embossed and decorated to add to the wearer's fierceness.

The Norman archers failed to make an appreciable indentation on the Saxon shield wall, because flights loosed uphill tended to stick in shields or go overhead. The Bayeux Tapestry shows axe and sword

'Fierce in attacking their enemies, ready to use guile'

Norman Knight

the sort of retribution described by Robert Wace, as one Housecarl:

'…Rushed straight upon a Norman knight who was armed and riding on a warhorse, and tried with his hatchet of steel to cleave his helmet; but the blow miscarried, and the sharp blade glanced down before the saddle-bow, driving through the horse's neck to the ground, so that both horse and master fell together to earth'.

Once down at the edge of the shield wall he was finished. The Bayeux Tapestry suggests the Norman knights were jabbing their lances over the top at those behind, riding by, especially vulnerable to being unhorsed by a whirling axe. Slowed down by the climb, stumbling horses were pushed away from the pliant shield wall, acting like an aggressive rugby scrum. Examination of surviving skeletons from the period reveals that most injuries appear to have been inflicted to the upper head and shoulder and lower pelvic region. Skull indentations suggest many fighters had no head protection at all. Injuries to the upper leg and pelvic region point to the common fighting practice of disabling with a spear thrust and then finishing off the victim as he tumbled to the ground, with a sword or axe blow to the head.[8]

The Normans were raiders, adept at swift mobile cavalry sweeps. Once elements of the Fyrd had been enticed beyond the shield wall by feigned retreats or cut off in groups, they were easy meat for the Norman horsemen. This mounted element and the employment of archers in support gave the Normans a greater degree of flexibility to whittle down the more immobile shield wall. Williams mounted command capability gave him an edge in this very tight contest between two evenly matched, tactically astute and ruthless warlords. It was a close run battle, lost with the fall of key commanders at crisis points. The Normans ventured all, planned cogently and won.

The Saxon shield Wall on the crest of Senlac Hill.

wielding Housecarls with clusters of arrows protruding from their shields. Cross-bows were employed at close ranges and these men, like the archers, occupied the lowliest social position in William's army. Hideous wounds caused by cross-bow quarrels against the unprotected Fyrd apparently caused real dismay in the depth of the English shield wall. It soon became apparent to the Normans that the only way to break through would be by direct attacks by mounted knights.

Norman war horses were carefully selected and bred stallions, taught to head-butt as well as kick and bite. They caused real consternation as the ground shook with their up canters against the shield lined hill-crest. Half a ton of horse and armoured rider could conceivably barge a breach in the shield wall, but horses shy away from seemingly solid objects. Attempting to simply push through, despite losing momentum invited

7. Malmsbury, KM Setton, Article *900 Years Ago. The Norman Conquest.* National Geographic, Aug 1966, P. 242.
8. Wounds, R.Kemp findings Stamford Bridge, interview R. Holmes *War Walks*, BBC TV 1997.

Facing the Saxon Shield Wall at Hastings 1066

THE HASTINGS BATTLEFIELD TOUR

The town of Battle where the battle of Hastings took place is 11 miles north-west of Hastings on the A2100, broadly the direction taken by William's army. On turning east along Telham Lane there is a track running north across Telham Hill offering the view the Normans would have first seen of Harold's army on Senlac Hill. This whole area was uncultivated heathland at the time. The clay valley between the two armies was swampy and undrained. Battle Abbey now stands on Senlac Hill, founded by William in about 1070 to atone for the considerable slaughter at the battle and the early part of his reign.

The English army approached its hill position moving south along the line of the A2100 north of Battle, pausing to muster during the final night at the hoar apple tree on Caldbec Hill. This is currently marked by a prominent white windmill. Harold moved to the hill crest along Battle High Street and the Whatlington Road.

Access to the English Heritage Visitor Centre and car park is off Battle High Street next to the Battle Abbey school grounds. The battle site is well marked with model tables that outline the course of the fighting and is used by this study. The National Heritage site includes the remaining open areas of Senlac Ridge and the grounds of the former abbey and valley bottom, where the Norman army formed up in three divisions for the assault. The wider area taken up by the English flight and the Malfosse ditch to the north is not within the National Heritage boundaries.

Battle Abbey stands roughly where Harold's banner was positioned, at the centre of the Senlac Hill crest-line.

① THE WEST END OF THE ENGLISH LINE

Battle Abbey protrudes into the original English line, which stretched west beyond the school grounds on its right, and east to the built up area on the left near the railway line. The professionals, Housecarls and Thegns, were at the front of the interlocking shield wall, with the Fyrd and freemen several ranks behind.

Robert Wace described the English peasant contingent *'bearing such arms as they found; clubs and great picks, iron forks and stakes'.*

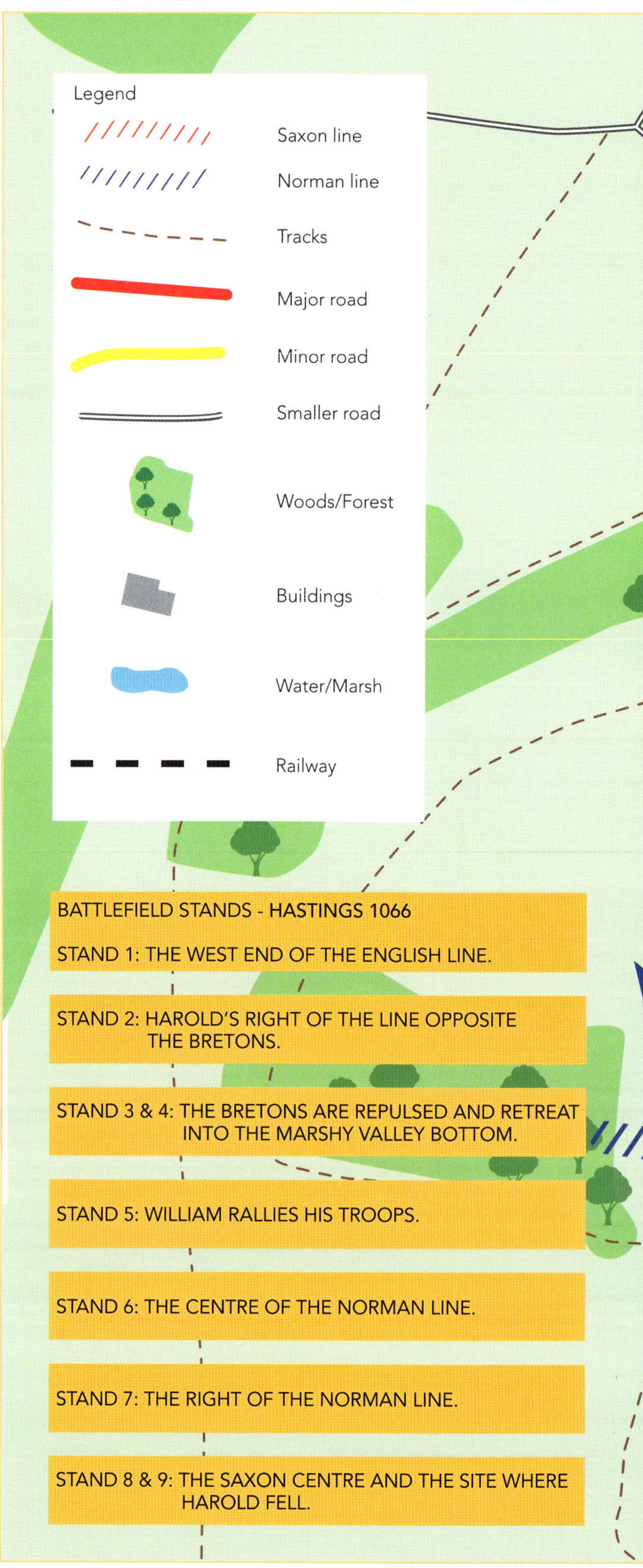

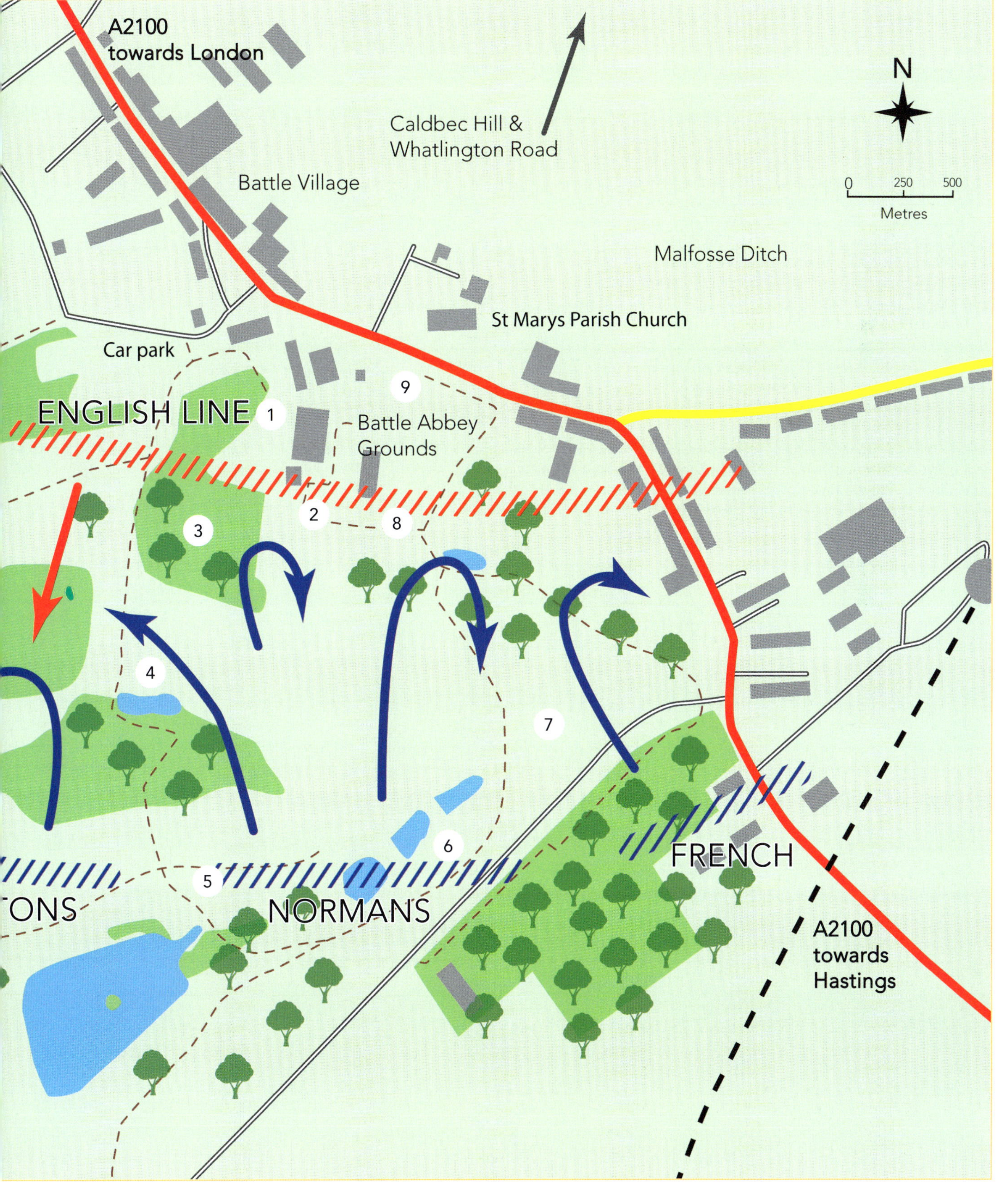

A2100
towards London
Caldbec Hill &
Whatlington Road
Battle Village
Malfosse Ditch
St Marys Parish Church
N
0   250   500
Metres
Car park
ENGLISH LINE
1
9
Battle Abbey
Grounds
2
8
3
4
7
6
5
TONS
NORMANS
FRENCH
A2100
towards
Hastings

Harold:

'…*Commanded the people, and counselled his barons to keep themselves all together and defend themselves in a body, for if they once separated, they would with difficulty recover themselves.*'

He warned that the shield wall must remain firm, saying:

'*The Normans are good vassals, valiant on foot and on horseback; good knights are they on horseback and well used to battle; all is lost if they once penetrate our ranks. They have brought long lances and swords, but you have pointed lances and keen edged bills [axes]; and I do not expect that their arms can stand against yours. Cleave whenever you can; it will be ill done if you spare aught*'.

William of Normandy was equally uncompromising, reminding his men that there was no going back, saying according to Wace:

'*There will be no safety in asking quarter or in flight; the English will never love or spare a Norman… Show no weakness towards them, for they will have no pity on you; neither the coward for running well, nor the bold man for smiting well, will be the better liked by the English, nor will any be the more spared on either account. You may fly to the sea, but you can fly no further; you will find neither ships nor bridge there; there will be no sailors to receive you, and the English will overtake you there and slay you in your shame. More of you will die in flight than in battle.*'[9]

The west side of the English line as viewed from an advancing Norman perspective

The Saxon view of the Norman army when it came into sight a mile away at Telham Hill in the far ground. The Normans advanced to the near ground in the grass valley bottom below, where it formed up into three divisions of three lines.

HAROLD'S RIGHT OF THE LINE OPPOSITE THE BRETONS

This position is reached by walking 100 yards along the line of the Abbey terrace. Observing half left with the Abbey School grounds behind offers an uninterrupted view of the Norman line as it advanced up the slope. William's chaplain, Chronicler William of Poitiers wrote:

'The Normans moved forward as follows in a well ordered line of battle, marching behind the standard which the Pope has given to them. In the first line William placed his infantry, armed with bows and arrows. In the second line he placed more infantry, better armed and wearing hauberks [coats of chain mail]. Behind them came the squadrons of cavalry, with William in the middle surrounded by the elite of his knights, so that he could send his orders in all directions, by hand signal and by shouting…The Duke and his men, in no way dismayed by the steep incline, began to advance slowly up the hill.'

The Bretons reached the English line first at this point and Robert Wace described how:

'Loud and far resounded the bray of the horns and the shocks of the lances, the mighty strokes of maces and the quick clashing of swords. One while the Englishmen rushed on, another while they fell back; one while the men from over sea charged onward, and again at other times retreated. 'The Normans shouted 'Dex Aie! [God Help!] the English people, 'Out!' Then came the cunning manoeuvres, the rude shocks and strokes of the lance and blows of the sword…'[10]

The Bretons are repulsed and stream back down the slope. [English Heritage].

The Normans strike the English line. 'Then came the cunning manoeuvres, the rude shocks and strokes of the lance and blows of the sword'.

THE BRETONS ARE REPULSED AND RETREAT INTO THE MARSHY VALLEY

Move back westward along the terrace and then follow the track downhill. Position three is reached by going through a group of trees through a gate to a model table. This is the area where the Bretons recoiled after hitting the shield wall. William of Poitiers wrote the English:

'…hurled their javelins and missiles of all sorts, they dealt savage blows with their axes and with stones hafted on wooden handles. You can well imagine how our men were crushed by these weapons, by this death-dealing onslaught. Then the knights rode forward, those who had hitherto been in support becoming the first line'.

Walk further down the slope with a fence to the right and pass a gorse-covered rough knoll. The area around the knoll was swampy and the small marsh-bounded pond is likely the furthest point the Bretons retreated before rallying. The cut-off Fyrd was butchered on and around the knoll. William of Poitiers described the turning of the Bretons on William's left:

'The Norman infantry turned in flight, terrified by this savage onslaught, and so did the knights from Brittany and the other auxiliaries on the left flank. Almost the whole of the battle-line of Duke William's fell back…The Normans imagined that their duke had fallen.'

9. Wace, *Le roman de Rou.*
10. Poitiers, *Deeds of William…*, *The Bayeux Tapestry and the Norman Invasion*, Thorpe translation, P. 48-9.

This is where William rallied the demoralised Breton left wing. The small bridge entering the area across the marshy land is to the left. The knoll was likely beneath the present day thick vegetation on the left.

5 WILLIAM RALLIES HIS TROOPS.

This position is further down the straight flight of wooden edged earth steps. Cross the small bridge on the northern end of a small lake, swing left, cross the bridge over the marshland and enter the swampy area where William managed to rally his demoralised left wing. Mounted soldiers charged in from the east (right) and slaughtered the vulnerable Fyrd dispersed in the open. They then massacred those who sought to resist from the knoll at position four further north. William of Poitiers chronicled the dramatic moment:

'When he [Duke William] *saw the greater part of the enemy force moving forward in pursuit, our leader rushed after his retreating troops, blocking those who were running away, bellowing at them and threatening them with his lance. He dragged off his helmet and showed them his bared head. 'Look at me!' he shouted. 'I am still alive! With God's help I shall win!…The Normans dashed back into battle, encircled the thousands* [an exaggeration] *who had pursued them and wiped them out in a moment so that there was not a single survivor'.*[11]

Harold missed this moment of opportunity, possibly because his two brothers fell at the same instant, which would have slowed momentum more than Williams's spirited rally.

6 THE CENTRE OF THE NORMAN LINE.

Position six is on the rising ground 200 yards off to the north-east. William commanded the battle from here; it affords a good view of the landscape and the entire English line. The top of the slope of Senlac Hill opposite has been terraced to accommodate the abbey buildings. Shaving the top off produced a gentler gradient from the discarded spoil. Robert Wace describes what was seen on that day in 1066, looking left and right as the Normans lined up for their first assault:

'The barons and knights and men-at-arms were all now armed; the foot soldiers were well equipped, each bearing bow and sword; on their heads were caps, and to their feet were bound buskins [a foot and leg cover reaching knee height, like a laced half-boot]. Some had good hides which they had bound round their bodies [for protection against blade slashes]; and many were clad in frocks, and had quivers and bows hung to their girdles.

The knights had hauberks and swords, boots of steel and shining helmets; shields at their necks and in their hands lances. And all had their cognizances [shield markings to distinguish the bearer] so that each might know his fellow, and Norman might not strike Norman, nor Frenchman kill his countryman by mistake. Those on foot led the way, with serried ranks, bearing their bows. The knights rode next, supporting the archers from behind. Thus both horse and foot kept their course and order of march as they began, in close ranks at a gentle pace, that the one might not pass or separate from the other. All went firmly and compactly, bearing themselves gallantly'. [12]

The centre of the Norman line after being repelled. [English Heritage]

The same view today viewed from the centre of the Norman line in the valley bottom, the abbey buildings surmount the crest, made gentler by the terracing effect.

Left: 'Look at me! I am still alive!' William bares his face to rally his troops as shown by the Bayeux Tapestry.

11. Poitiers, Ibid, P. 49 and 50.
12. Wace, *Le roman de Rou*.

 7 THE RIGHT OF THE NORMAN LINE.

Continuing right along the path for another 200 yards gives an oblique view of the English centre, so tenaciously held and given up only yard by yard. The slope would have been steeper and covered in gorse and heath at the time. William of Poitiers describes the ruses employed to draw some of the more unstable Fyrd away from Harold's shield wall on the crest line:

'Now that the barbarians seemed to be on the point of victory, they were filled with great exaltation. They shouted to each other and a great cry went up as they hurled insults at our men, threatening to overrun them without more ado. As had happened on the previous occasion, some thousand or more of the English [an over-estimate] rushed boldly forward, thinking to harass those who were running away. Suddenly the Normans turned their horses, cut off the force which was pursuing them, made a complete circle around them and massacred them to the last man'.

The complete line ahead, left and right was locked in a bloody stalemate for hours. William of Poitiers explained the English:

'…fought with all their might, their great objective being to avoid a breach being made in their line by those who were assailing them. They were so densely massed that the men who were killed could hardly fall to the ground. However, gaps began to appear in their ranks here and there, where the iron weapons of our brave soldiers were having their effect…The English battle-line was still terrifying to behold and the Normans had great difficulty in containing it… The Normans shot their arrows, brandished their swords, transfixed the enemy with their spears. The dead as they tumbled to the ground, showed more sign of motion than the living. The serried mass of their companions prevented those who were lightly wounded from withdrawing, so tightly were they grouped together'.[13]

8 9 THE SAXON CENTRE AND THE SITE WHERE HAROLD FELL.

Position eight is on the terrace at the crest of the hill in front of Battle Abbey. About 150 yards north of the shell of the abbey building is the first site of the alter where Harold allegedly fell. The buildings obstruct the symmetry of the 1066 scene, which would have been a plateau beyond the crest-line, where isolated knots of Housecarls, Thegns and Fyrd fought to the death. The *Carmen de Hastingae Proelio* or 'Song of the Battle of Hastings', probably written by Bishop Guy of Amiens, tells the story of Harold's grisly end at the hands of four Norman knights. Whether or not he had been disabled by an arrow in the eye is not clear. Only his mistress Edith Swaneck was able to pick out his remains, guided by a lover's eye.

'With the point of his lance the first [Norman knight] pierced Harold's shield and then penetrated his chest, drenching the ground with his blood, which poured out in torrents. With his sword the second cut off his head, just below where his helmet protected him. The third disembowelled him with his javelin. The fourth hacked off his leg at the thigh [a euphemism for possible castration] and hurled it far away. Struck down in this way, his dead body lay on the ground'.

William of Poitiers described the English retreat, conducted all around and beyond the present day abbey, scattering to the north:

'The English turned in flight and made off at full speed, some on the horses which they had seized, others on foot, some along the

This view taken left oblique from the right of the Norman line shows the Saxon centre and left, giving a fine impression of the slope of Senlac Hill.

Below: This monument erected to commemorate the bravery of both sides stands near the inscribed slab that marks the spot where Harold allegedly died.

Above: The shield wall was subjected to volleys of arrow fire throughout the battle. [English Heritage].

trackways, most of them through the pathless desert [heath land]. *Bathed in their blood, they struggled to escape, while others dragged themselves to their feet but could not walk a step. Their frantic desire to escape gave new strength to some. Many died where they dropped in the deep recesses of the woods; and even more were discovered by those in pursuit where they had fallen along the trackways. Although the country was unknown to them, the Normans pursued the English relentlessly, cutting the fugitives down…'*

Chronicler William of Malmesbury comments that the Norman pursuers did not have it all their own way. Six hundred yards north of Caldbec Hill was a precipitous gully hidden in the approaching gloom by brambles and undergrowth. This Malfosse or 'evil ditch' could be the Oakwood Gill, a ravine on the edge of the present day Duniford Wood. It became a salutary check for the elated Normans hunting down fugitives, because as the leading riders tumbled into the ditch, newly arrived Housecarls or retreating Saxons turned on them.

'Nor indeed were they at all wanting to their own revenge, as, by frequently making a stand, they slaughtered their pursuers in heaps: for, getting possession of an eminence, [slope] they drove down the Normans, when roused with English indignation…into the valley beneath, where, easily hurling their javelins and rolling down stones on them as they stood below, they destroyed them to a man'.[14]

Never underestimate the English. William was to rule England, like Normandy, with a rod of iron.

13. Poitiers, Ibid, P.51.
14. Carmen…, P. Marren, *1066*, P. 140. Poitiers, Ibid, P. 53. Malmesbury, Regnum Anglorum, Ed W. Stubbs 1887.

'Middle Earth' fantasy versus Medieval brutality – filming Hastings 1066

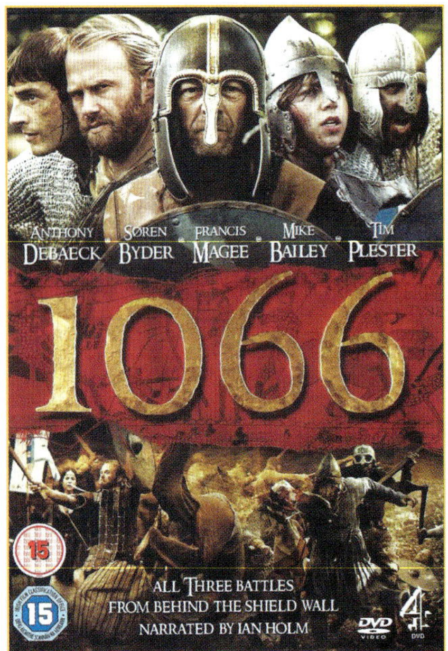

1066: THE BATTLE FOR MIDDLE EARTH (2009)

1066: The Battle For Middle Earth belies its unfortunate Hobbit-like sub-title and offers an original approach to the three momentous battles that were fought that year. The two-part dramatic historical re-enactment is not about the kings but views events through the medieval visor of soldiers in the ranks. Directed by Justin Hardy and written by Peter Harness, it was broadcast on British Channel 4 TV in May 2009.

The first instalment covers the Viking invasion of Harald Hardrada in the North of England. The northern Saxon earls are defeated at Fulford but Harold Godwinson, who had been poised on the southern coastline anticipating a Norman invasion quickly conducts an epic march to the north. This is seen through the eyes of the 'weapons men' recruited from the village of Crowhurst local to Hastings. He beats the Vikings decisively at Stamford Bridge, whereupon the soldiers hear that the Normans have landed in the south. The second part of the film deals with the exhausting return march, the sacking of their home village by the rapacious Normans and the hard fought defeat at

Hastings. It was beautifully filmed at Bolton Abbey and Flamborough Head in Yorkshire and parts of Sussex in 2008.

Hardy follows a microcosm of Anglo-Saxon experience by following the fortunes of the peasant soldiers from the Sussex village of Crowhurst. His researchers had discovered that the village had been 'laid to waste' according to the Domesday Book, compiled after William's successful invasion. This 11th Century source provided the scenario around which Hardy could develop a dramatic sequence of events centring on the common people. Their fortunes are imaginatively followed using sociological detail provided by extracts from the Norse Sagas, Domesday Book, Bayeux Tapestry and the *Carmen de Hastingae*, the vivid contemporary song of the battle of Hastings. Only Harold Godwinson is included in any meaningful way, the rest of the cast are fictional characters.

The story centres upon a 14-year old Crowhurst newly-wed called Tofi (played by Mike Baily) interacting with his friend Leofric (Tim Plester), a cowardly farmer who becomes a Housecarl warrior. Ordgar (Francis Magee) the local Housecarl and professional warrior is charged with recruiting and leading the village's able-bodied men in the English army. They confront the Vikings at Stamford Bridge and recruit one of their number, Snorri (played convincingly by

The Housecarl Warrior Ordgar (Francis Magee). [Channel 4]

The Crowhurst Fyrd at the shield Wall. [Channel 4]

The Saxons attack at Stamford Bridge. [Channel 4]

The film gives a flavour of the terrors and hardships felt by those in the ranks of the Medieval armies. [Channel 4]

Søren Byder) to fight alongside the English before the nemesis at Hastings. Here they confront the cruel and ruthless Norman war leader Ozouf (Anthony Debaeck) and the nobler and more humane Coutances (Peter Guiness) across the shield wall at Hastings.

These roles are played with varying success and authenticity. The Norman and Viking leads have an air of grainy authenticity about them but the characters are a little caricatured. Anglo-Saxons are portrayed as rustic and wimpish up against lethal rock-hard and weather-beaten Vikings. The supposedly fearsome Housecarl Ordgar, who roars about lopping off enemy limbs, is dismissed in one Guardian *1066* blog as having the demeanour of a 'bad tempered pub landlord'. Fulsome moustaches and shaggy beards are conspicuously absent from the Saxon Housecarls portrayed whereas half-shaven Norman heads do promote sinister 'ork' qualities that differentiate them as alien foreign invaders. Intermittent screen excerpts showing historical source notes to explain some action sequences promotes a degree of historical authenticity as also the detail of traditional *Destrier* horses ridden by some of the Norman knights. The epic march north and south conducted by the Crowhurst Fyrd on foot was unlikely to have happened. Harold and his core of Housecarl professionals rode, joining with northern levees at Stamford Bridge and riding back to join the southern Fyrdmen at London and Hastings.

The 'Middle Earth' Tolkien terminology employed in the script is more appropriate to the *Lord of the Rings* trilogy and is out of place in a serious historical epic. Seeking perhaps to capitalise on the Ring genre for publicity and promotion purposes, it comes across as laboured style. Referring to the Normans as 'Orks' and the English Channel as the 'Whale Road', with soldiers distracted by 'elves' on the line of march stretches Tolkien's Anglo-Saxon antecedents (he was a lecturer at Oxford), too far. He taught Anglo-Saxon language, but the fantasy interpretation of historical sources in the same Norse-myths vein distracts from what was essentially a brutal contest between the English and a rapacious Norman invader. Ian Holmes narrative also strays into this melodramatic pseudo-fantasy mould and is at odds with the more realistic aspects of the film.

1066 certainly gives a flavour of the hardships and terror experienced by those serving in the ranks of the medieval armies. Hundreds of extras from the *Regia Anglorum* Hastings battle re-enactment group supported by a stunt-team admirably bulk-out Hardy's small cast. Despite the appalling weather encountered during the battle shoots, the shield walls, thumping impacts of volleys of arrows and Norman cavalry charges are gripping and historically authentic. The muted colours of the photography and

The grim totality of the English defeat at Hastings portrayed in 1066. [Channel 4]

costumes add to the realism of the close-in battle scenes. Up to an hour of this epic consists of battle shoots that vividly reveal the viscerally violent feel of battle as experienced by the common soldier.

Justin Hardy's film is a gripping historical drama that is broadly successful in showing the microcosm of medieval common experience it purports to show. It accurately follows the sequence of events that the few historical sources relate about the course of the battle. It is well worth viewing and stands alone as the only epic film that has attempted to cover the battle of Hastings in 1066.

THE COUNTDOWN TO THE
100 DAYS CAMPAIGN

Napoleon risked all near Grenoble in March 1815, when royalist forces sent to arrest him on return from exile refused to open fire. One month later he was back in power at Paris and the 100-Day campaign clock began. [Calvin Bullock Collection]

Europe was at peace in February 1815 after 23 years of unbroken war. Napoleon Bonaparte the self-appointed emperor of France was interned on Elba, an inconsequential island 140 miles off the coast of Corsica in the Mediterranean, a humiliating end for the victor of fifty battles. For ten months Napoleon shrewdly monitored French popular opinion on the mainland, increasingly critical of the puppet Bourbon King Louis XVIII, installed after his departure. As the Allied powers bickered over the future of defeated France at the Congress of Vienna, Napoleon seized his chance and escaped on the 16th February.

He embarked over one thousand grenadiers from his personal battalion of the Imperial Guard in six small ships, alongside a handful of lancers, two cannon, three accompanying generals and a carriage loaded with gold coins. Napoleon's small convoy reached Golfe Juan on the coast of southern France, part of modern day Cannes. He had characteristically gambled and won. 'If they'd kept a frigate in the harbour and another outside' he later said 'it would have been impossible for me to have gone to France'.[1]

He began the 800 kilometre march north-west to Paris with just over 1,000 men. The first test of loyalties came on the 7th March at the narrow defile that guards the southern route into the town of Grenoble near Lake Laffrey. Blocking Napoleon's route was a royalist force of six infantry regiments and hussars. Shouted exchanges of 'We are all Frenchmen!' and 'If you fire on the Emperor you will be responsible to all of France' signalled an impasse. Napoleon approached the opposing vanguard, a solitary figure in his distinctive greatcoat and cocked hat, relying on his personal charisma to carry the day. *'Fire!'* shrieked a young officer, but nobody dared shoot. 'If there is any man among you who wants to kill his Emperor' Napoleon gravely announced as he unbuttoned his famous grey greatcoat, 'here I am'. There were none. A solitary voice yelled *'Vive l'Empereur!'* and the triumphal procession continued on its way, joined by ever more units and former marshals as they progressed.

Napoleon was back in power on 29th April 1815 having set off with a single battalion from the southern coast on the 1st March he arrived with two divisions. He now proceeded to build an army. The Congress of Vienna proclaimed Napoleon an outlaw on the same day and declared war on the man, not France. The hundred day campaign clock had started to tick.

The French planned to concentrate small numbers of divisions to oppose and delay their nearest enemies from behind natural border barriers. Napoleon intended to strike with his largest force – the Armée du Nord – before the allies could mobilise and join together. By the 14th June Napoleon had concentrated the 123,000 soldiers of the Army of the North with 246 artillery pieces in an area of 18 square kilometres around his headquarters at Beaumont near the Belgian border. There were advantages to defend rather than attack after only two months of being back in imperial control. Napoleon preferred to gamble and grasp the political and military advantages that would accrue from an immediate spoiling attack.

Arthur Wellesley, the Duke of Wellington and victor of the Spanish Peninsula campaign against Napoleon was placed in

During the early hours of the 14th June Napoleon unexpectedly invaded Belgium.[Musee de l'Armée]

command of the Anglo-Allied army. On leaving the Congress at Vienna Tsar Alexander of Russia laid his hand on his shoulder and declared 'It is for you to save the world again'. The combined Anglo-Allied, Prussian, Austrian, Russian and Italian armies numbered 800,000 and had agreed to invade France and converge on Paris. The French could only counter with 250,000 soldiers overall. The Allies had first to mobilise. Only two of their armies, Wellington's and Blücher's Prussian army were in the field in the spring of 1815, ready to face the French.

Wellington's forces were stationed in an arc south west of Brussels with Blucher's army forming the other end of the semi-circle to the south east of the city. Nobody really knew what was going on in Paris or whether Napoleon intended to attack or defend. Not knowing where the blow might fall produced wide dispersion acerbated by logistics. Wellington's line of communications for his 112,000 strong army around Brussels, pointed north-west towards Ostend and the sea, Blücher's supply lines for his 130,000 strong Prussian army at Namur extended east to the Rhine. Both had agreed to cooperate and were confident 'to do the business' whatever strategy Bonaparte adopted. Wellington suspected Napoleon might go west around Mons to cut him off from the sea and the Royal Navy, his traditional haven in Portugal.

The French unexpectedly invaded Belgium during the early hours of 14th June. Three columns crossed the River Sambre near Charleroi in pouring rain and drove back the surprised Prussian outposts. The Charleroi region was the 'hinge' or key point linking Blücher's forward outposts with Wellington, their respective headquarters at Namur and Brussels were 64 kilometres apart. The left wing of Napoleon's Armée du Nord edged up the Brussels road towards Quatre-Bras, while his main force pushed up the Liége road towards Ligny on the right. Napoleon had split the Allied line at its centre. Napoleon later recalled:

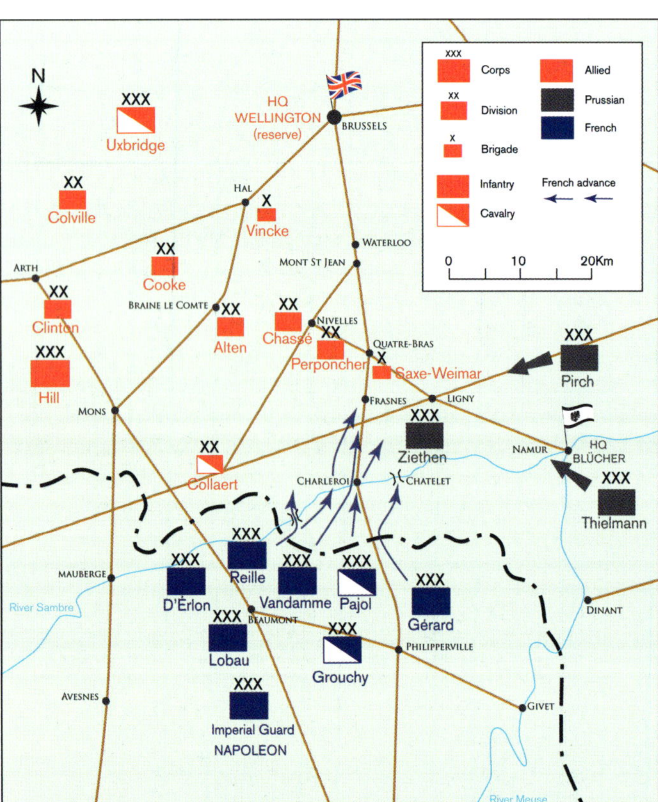

Napoleon launched his invasion into Belgium on 15th June 1815, his army unexpectedly emerging between Wellington's Anglo-Allied forces and Blücher's Prussians. The French subdivided into two wings for the approach on Brussels, the left wing taking the road to Quatre-Bras, the right to Ligny.

'The two enemy armies were taken by surprise, their communications already considerably embarrassed. All my manoeuvres had succeeded as I wished. I could now take the initiative of attacking the enemy armies one by one'.

The more 'brutal' Blücher, Napoleon reasoned, would be more energetic hastening to aid his ally, than the 'cold' and calculating Wellington. *'All my measures had therefore'* Napoleon concluded, *'the objective of attacking the Prussians first'.*[2]

Napoleon's phantom strategy of false intelligence, suggesting he would thrust to the Belgian coast had been successful. Wellington's defensive posture was leaning towards Mons as Napoleon hammered in the wedge dislocating the 'hinge' between the two Allied armies at Charleroi. The French had stolen a 24 hour march on the allies, who it was thought would need three days to mass.

Wellington's heterogeneous Anglo-Allied Army, unlike Napoleon's purely French veteran core, had seven nationalities in all, eight including the Prussians. The force was infantry-heavy, with 53,850 foot soldiers compared to 13,350 cavalry, or about one in four. He had 157 guns and howitzers, nearly 90 less than the French. The Prussian army of the Lower Rhine, pushed aside by Napoleon's unexpected appearance, had three-corps with 130,000 men and 304 guns. Although large, more than half the force was composed of *Landwehr* or militia troops, many of whom had been recruited outside Prussia itself.

Blücher was defeated at Ligny on 16th June, despite outnumbering the French by 93,000 to 66,000. Napoleon waited in vain for the arrival of Comte d'Érlon's I Corps, due to outflank the Prussians before breaking through the Prussian centre. D'Érlon had been diverted by a confusing mix of orders from closing on Wellington at Quatre-Bras and missed both engagements. The result was a severe mauling for the Prussians rather than outright victory for the French. Blücher's IV Corps also failed to arrive in time and missed the battle. Despite the severity of the reversal at Ligny, the Prussian retreat was well managed, but it lost nearly 10,000 deserters retreating north to Wavre during the night.

Napoleon felt he had victory in his grasp. *'The Prussian losses were enormous'*, he later wrote, *'six of their corpses could be seen for every French corpse'.* Marshal Grouchy's corps was despatched late, to finish the Prussians off, but lost contact with them.

The small hamlet of Quatre-Bras, was as the name suggests, a crossroads 38 kilometres south of Brussels. It formed part of the vital hinge between the two armies that Napoleon sought to dislocate. Wellington, caught off balance by Napoleon's rapid advance was trying to move his forces eastward as rapidly as possible to support the Prussians. He had promised Blücher, on the morning of the 16th at Ligny, that the rest of his army should reach Genappe and Nivelles nearby by noon, but his staff's calculations proved wildly over optimistic.

Prussian General Gneisenau gives the order to retreat. The Prussian Army suffered a serious reverse at Ligny on 16th June, but managed to break free of the pursuing French. [Historiches Museum Rastatt]

Wellington, seen here at Quatre Bras alongside his retreating troops and French prisoners, fought an inconclusive meeting battle with the French on the 16th June. His army had to fall back towards Brussels during a torrential summer storm, to maintain contact with the Prussians, on his left flank. [Ernst Croft]

Marshall Ney commanding the left wing advanced Reille's 20,000 men corps against Wellington and by early afternoon on the 16th they were penetrating the head-high crops and woods adjoining the cross roads at Quatre-Bras. Ney was confident, that D'Érlon's additional 20,000 men would arrive any moment. His attack had only to secure the wooded area of the Bois de Bossu on the road leading north to Brussels and the city would be theirs. The battle, however, degenerated into a 'come as you are' meeting engagement for both sides. Each new unit was just sufficient on arrival to stave off defeat, and this continued all afternoon. When Ney attacked at 14.30 the Anglo-Allies could only muster 8,000 against his 28,000. Picton's 5th Division arrived at 15.00 and two hours later Alten's 3rd Division turned up from Nivelles, while the Brunswickers and Nassauers came in from Brussels. The steady build up achieved parity at 26,000 and then absolute superiority when over 30,000 allies had arrived. The luckless D'Érlon marched and counter

DID THE APPALLING WEATHER ON THE EVE OF WATERLOO CHANGE THE COURSE OF HISTORY?

The decade 1810 to 1819 had been the coldest since the 1690s. Meteorological records indicate that June 1815 was the wettest month of the year in England. The log books of the English Channel Fleet at Ostend record the violent summer storm that occurred on 17th/18th June and notes that it was followed by drier conditions after a wet start to the day.

Professor Laurent Bock from the University of Gembloux recently conducted a soil survey at Waterloo, which showed the soil on Wellington's ridge would have become firm quite quickly. French positions down in the valley where Ney's cavalry formed up would have remained water-logged. Soil conditions favoured Wellington's defence. If Napoleon had waited, it would have taken three or four days for the ground ➤

Mud delayed the arrival of the heavy 12-pounder French artillery, vital for the Grand Battery's preparatory bombardment. The roads had been turned into a quagmire. [FJ Gueldry]

to dry out. Delaying for a few hours made little difference, the field remained a quagmire.

Victor Hugo argued that Divine intervention caused Napoleon's downfall, claiming in his novel *Les Misérables* that *'had it not rained on the night of the 17th/18th June 1815, the future of Europe would have been different'.* The point is often made that Napoleon delayed the start of the battle because the wet ground impeded the movement forward of the Grand Battery's potential battle-winning heavy 12-pounders. Delay provided time for the Prussian army to unite with Wellington and inflict the critical blow just when the outcome of the battle was delicately balanced.

Rain the night before meant muskets had to be 'boiled out' with hot water to remove residual powder and carbon deposits. This, and physical discomfort verging on exposure for tired soldiers, affected both armies. The summer storm cloaked the retreat of the Allied armies during the night before Waterloo. Mud was to impede the deployment of artillery and cavalry on both sides the next day. It did nullify the impact of Napoleon's artillery superiority, reducing the bounce of round-shot on the soft ground, but Wellington's decision to deploy behind the Mont St Jean ridgeline probably did most to reduce the vulnerability of troops to cannon fire. Napoleon's army took a long time to form up, but delays were caused just as much by poor march discipline and the need to forage locally for food that morning than muddy conditions. Only the Imperial Guard had its own integral logistic wagon train. Nor was Napoleon galvanised by any knowledge that the Prussians were already marching to Wellington's assistance.

The primary impact of the weather on this battle was that the hot afternoon following the wet cold night produced atmospheric conditions that added to battlefield obscuration

British soldiers fall back from Quatre-Bras covered by a violent summer storm that was to turn the battlefield into a soggy morass. [Columbia Pictures]

through mist and hanging smoke. By mid afternoon Napoleon could not see into the valley. This might have influenced the premature release of the French cavalry, which was to confront solid infantry squares instead of the retreat that Marshal Ney was convinced he saw happening through the smoke beyond the ridgeline. Napoleon could not see how weak Wellington's centre was when La Haye-Sainte

fell and neither could he probably encompass the true extent of Prussian numbers entering the field.

In short, the vagaries of the weather impacted on both sides but likely favoured Wellington's intrinsic advantage of holding the high ground in defence; a less vulnerable option and tactically far less demanding than the French need to attack.

---

marched all day without confronting anyone. Wellington managed to shore up his crumbling line and Blücher escaped an even worse mauling, perhaps decisive defeat. Nevertheless, Napoleon had the initiative; having worsted the Prussians he was convinced he would brush Wellington aside in the morning and enter Brussels.

One year before Wellington had ridden the open ground in front of the Forest of Soignes near the village of Waterloo. He saw it to be a favourable potential defensive position. An engineer's survey was commissioned to produce a map of the surrounding area to record his findings. From here, Wellington felt he could block the road to Brussels, if Blücher could support him 'even with one corps only'. Wellington remarked to an aide on hearing about the Prussian reverse at Ligny that *'Old Blücher has had a damned good licking and gone back to Wavre, eighteen miles'.* This meant his left flank at Quatre-Bras was in the air. *'As he has gone back, we must go too'* he concluded.

The withdrawal was screened by the newly arrived British cavalry. A violent summer storm engulfed both armies as the

soldiers retreated through driving rain across 20 kilometres of difficult roads, knee-deep in glutinous mud. After four to six hours of forced marches conducted amid the sounds of rear-guard skirmishing behind them Wellington's infantry columns began to cross the La Belle Alliance ridge on the road to Waterloo village. *'As soon as the troops reached that part of the road, nearest to the farmhouse of La Haye Sainte'*, British Private Thomas Morris with the 73rd Regiment recalled, *'the different brigades filed off to the right or left to take up their respective positions'.*[3] It was clear that they would stand here.

The French closed up behind and deployed about a mile and a half away. They were confident they could brush aside this small British rear-guard in the morning.

1. Peter Snow, *To War With Wellington*, P.246.
2. Napoleon, *The Waterloo Campaign*, P. 81 and 73-4.
3. Morris, ed J Selby, *Thomas Morris*, P. 73.

A Near Run Thing

THE BATTLE OF WATERLOO
18TH JUNE 1815

On the 18th June 1815 Wellington and Napoleon's two armies faced each other across separate ridges twelve miles south of Brussels. The battlefield was small. It measured two and a quarter miles deep from north to south, where the Brussels road intersected the La Belle Alliance and Mont St Jean ridgelines and four miles wide. Napoleon waited until late morning for the ground to dry out after raining all night, so that he could move his heavy cannon. The Prussian army under General Blücher had departed Wavre ten miles away to join with Wellington. What should have taken six-hours of forced marching to achieve lasted nearly all day, because of the soggy undulating ground they had to cross.

Wellington's army of 90,000 faced Napoleon's 107,500. Both had sizable contingents elsewhere. Wellington had 17,000 men at Hal to screen his westward line of communications to Ostend, while Napoleon had 30,000 men under Marshal Grouchy chasing Blücher to Wavre. Blücher was inbound with 75,000 troops of which 49,000 would arrive in the nick of time, leaving 25,000 to counter Grouchy. Wellington held the line with 73,000 troops from eight nations of which about one third were British, against Napoleon's 77,500 veteran Frenchmen.

PHASE 1: THE OPENING SHOTS AT HOUGOUMONT

At 11.30 the French Grand Battery opened fire and the fighting, which can be usefully broken down into five phases, began. It would continue until about 20.00. Napoleon had little room for tactical manoeuvre; he was constrained by woodland to left and right. He chose to hammer away at the centre of Wellington's line until he broke through to Brussels. Two fortified farm complexes at the right and centre of Wellington's line, at Hougoumont and La Haye Sainte, had the effect of impeding and channelling direct mass attacks. The line ended at a third farm at Papalotte to the east, where the Prussians were anticipated to appear.

Phase 1 began with a feint attack by Reille's French II Corps against the fortified and wooded hamlet at the Chateau Hougoumont. This was meant to divert attention from Napoleon's main point of effort, a four-infantry division-strong attack by D'Érlon's I Corps at the centre of the Anglo-Allied line. From the start, this diversion soaked up more French than Allied forces. The tenacious and epic defence of Hougoumont by the British Guards, soon set on fire, was to last the entire day.

The battle opened with intense fighting for the Chateau Hougoumont. (Re-enactment).

The following 3D images are based on top-relief diagrams charting the course of the action at Battle of Waterloo 1815

Phase 1. 11.30.
The battle opens with Reille's infantry assault on the British held farm at Hougoumont to the right of Wellington's line.

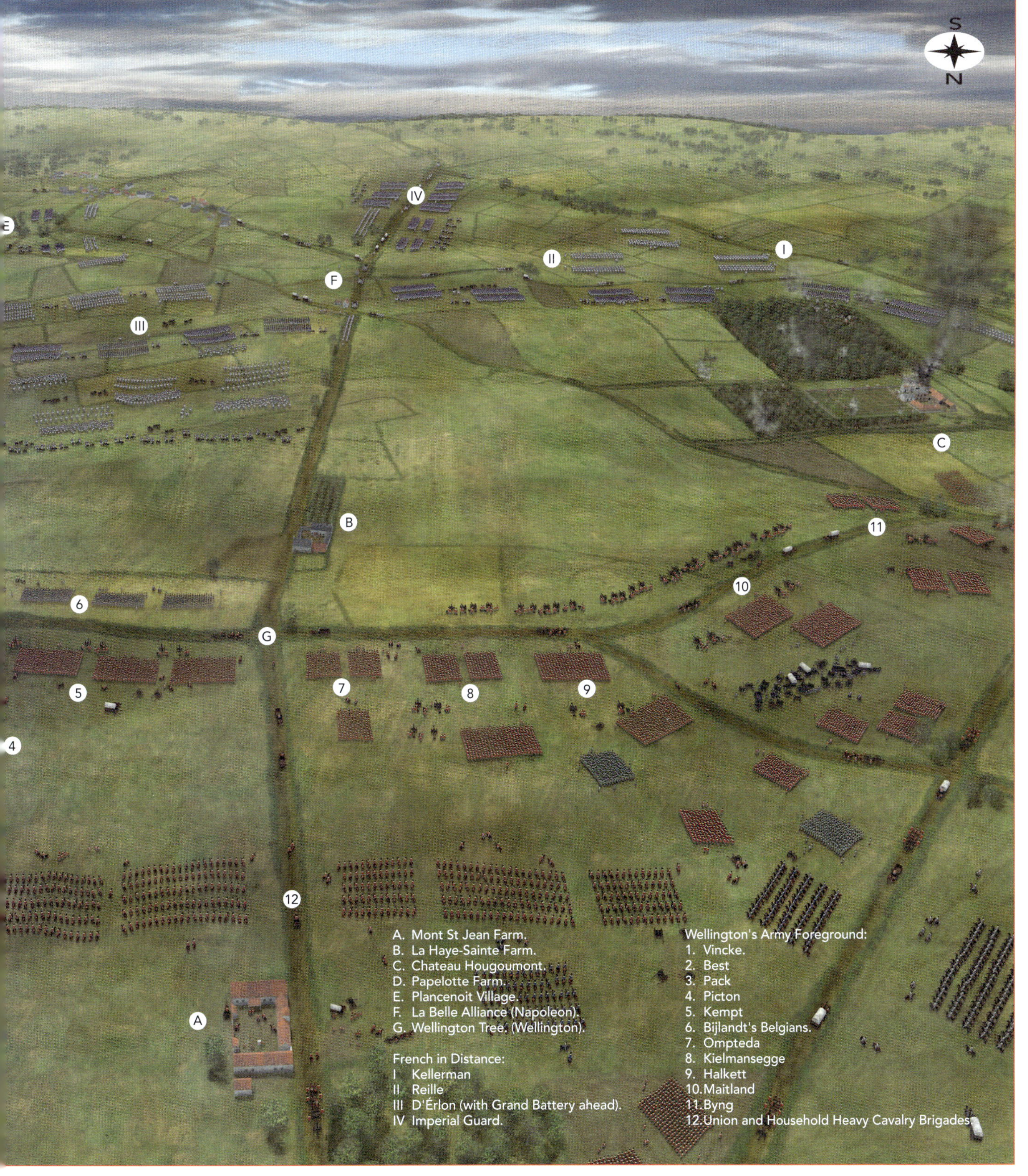

A. Mont St Jean Farm.
B. La Haye-Sainte Farm.
C. Chateau Hougoumont.
D. Papelotte Farm.
E. Plancenoit Village.
F. La Belle Alliance (Napoleon).
G. Wellington Tree. (Wellington).

French in Distance:
I   Kellerman
II Reille
III D'Érlon (with Grand Battery ahead).
IV Imperial Guard.

Wellington's Army Foreground:
1. Vincke.
2. Best
3. Pack
4. Picton
5. Kempt
6. Bijlandt's Belgians.
7. Ompteda
8. Kielmansegge
9. Halkett
10. Maitland
11. Byng
12. Union and Household Heavy Cavalry Brigades

PHASE 2: THE MASS FRENCH INFANTRY ASSAULT

A storm of artillery fire from the French Grand Battery announced the start of phase 2, which was a massive infantry assault against the centre of the Mont Saint-Jean ridge by D'Érlon's infantry corps. Four huge columns of French infantry reached the crest of the ridge despite a pounding from Allied cannon. A Dutch-Belgian brigade was swept aside creating a gap in the line, which was filled by Picton's 5th British Division out of sight behind the ridgeline. As the French columns were suddenly checked by concentrated musket fire, delivered in extended line, two British heavy brigades of cavalry led by the Earl of Uxbridge swept into their flanks with consummate timing. Their totally unexpected appearance put the French to flight but the reckless British cavalry over-reached themselves. After penetrating the Grand Battery to their front they were enfiladed by a French cavalry counter-stroke and largely destroyed as a coherent fighting force. Both sides suffered heavy casualties and were back at their start points. Time was running out for Napoleon, who had meanwhile spotted the approaching Prussians.

'The pace quickened'. French infantry in the attack. [Re-enactment]

Phase 2. 14.00.
D'Érlon attacks the allied centre to the right of the cross-roads and is repelled by the British heavy cavalry brigades.

The gap in the line was plugged by Picton's Highlanders'.

PHASE 3: REPEATED ATTACKS BY MASSED FRENCH CAVALRY.

Marshal Ney mistook Wellington's readjustment of his battered forces for a retreat and ordered in the cavalry to exploit the development. This ushered in phase 3, the great French cavalry attacks, which started at about 16.00. They covered the whole area between La Haye Sainte and Hougoumont. Unsupported by infantry and with no utensils to spike any Allied cannon they overran, Ney's cavalry broke the line only to repeatedly dash themselves against unbroken infantry squares. As many as 12 attacks were raked by the same guns brought into action again by crews who had sheltered inside the squares. By 18.00 both sides were exhausted.

Wellington's centre line was terribly battered and virtually without reserves. He personally led forward the Brunswickers to restore the centre. Meanwhile von Bülow's IV Prussian Corps arrived and spent the next four hours contesting the village of Plancenoit on Napoleon's right flank.

Masses of French cavalry filled the open ground between La Haye Sainte and Hougoumont. (Detail. Waterloo Panorama).

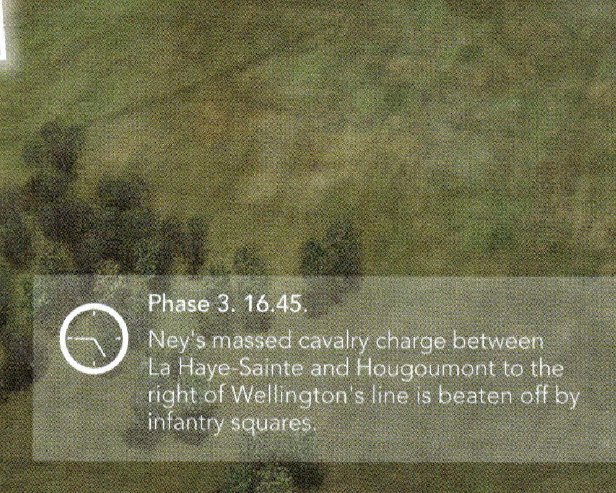

French cavalry in the attack. [Re-enactment].

PHASE 4: THE FALL OF LA HAYE SAINTE AND A TEETERING ALLIED CENTRE.

Phase 4 began with the collapse of the farm complex at La Haye Sainte. The blazing building was defended to the last by the King's German Legion but was overrun by D'Érlon's infantry, directed by Ney.

This was perhaps Wellington's most dangerous moment. The Allied centre was threatening to give way and the Prussian arrival had been checked at Plancenoit village. Wellington's army was being steadily worn down, but Napoleon uncharacteristically failed to reinforce the success Ney had created at this point.

The Allied centre was under acute French pressure, French infantry in the attack.

Phase 4. 18.30.
Ney attacks and captures La Haye-Sainte, threatening to finally pierce the Allied line.

Only disciplined British infantry fire-power kept the French at bay.

PHASE 5: THE FINAL ASSAULT AND REPULSE OF NAPOLEON'S ELITE IMPERIAL GUARD.

The final phase of the battle began at about 19.00 when Napoleon brought forward his final reserve, the Imperial Guard. They had never lost a battle to date being only ever inserted at the point of victory. The Guard attacked diagonally towards Wellington's right centre, between Hougoumont - still holding out - and La Haye Sainte, which had fallen. Like D'Érlon's failed infantry attack, the Guard columns were packed too tightly to deploy against concentrated British musket fire.

The Imperial Guard floundered in the face of volley fire from Maitland's brigade of Guards and an unexpected assault on its left flank by the 52nd Light Infantry. As the French were repulsed the Prussians were emerging in ever greater numbers from the left of Wellington's line. Caught in a closing vice, when Wellington ordered a general advance at 20.00, the French retreat turned into a rout.

Wellington won because of superior tactics and the timely arrival of the Prussians. He took advantage of the dead ground behind the Mont Saint-Jean ridge to conceal his forces and reduce their vulnerability to superior French cannon fire. Tightly compacted advancing French columns were broken by concentrated infantry musket fire and crippled by decisive cavalry attacks. Napoleon's traditional column and line tactics were constrained by the narrowness of the battlefield, acerbated by the fortified bastions at Hougoumont and La Haye Sainte, which broke up the scale of the attacks. French infantry and cavalry did not adequately coordinate and support each other, a failure of leadership, despite the superiority of their artillery.

Even Napoleon's elite Imperial Guard, who had never lost a battle, failed to penetrate the Allied line.

Phase 5. 19.30.

The final advance of Napoleon's Imperial Guard to the right of Wellington's line is repelled and the French begin to retreat, assailed on their right by the Prussians entering the field in ever greater numbers from the east.

Wellington: The Consumate
Professional

THE DUKE OF WELLINGTON

Napoleon on the eve of Waterloo was to confront Arthur Wellesley, the Duke of Wellington for the first time. His Marshals urged caution, but Napoleon brutally put them down. *'Because you have been beaten by Wellington, you consider him a great general' he criticised, 'now I tell you that Wellington is a bad general, that the English are bad troops'*. So far as he was concerned *ce sera l'affaire d'un déjeuner*, literally 'This'll be a picnic'. His marshals remained dubious, *'I earnestly hope so'* responded his Chief of Staff Marshal Soult.[4]

Wellington, born in 1769, came from an impoverished Anglo-Irish gentry family. His background made him a driven man. He was rejected by the Pakenham family as 'not up to scratch' when he courted his future wife Kitty, which made him determined to prove otherwise. She took on the status of an objective won alongside his considerable military reputation by 1806, but by then she had *'grown ugly by Jove!'* [5]

After first purchasing a commission, Wellesley's army rise was meteoric, from Ensign at the age of 16 to Lieutenant Colonel and commander of the 33rd Regiment by 24. Once his brother secured the Governer-Generalship of India in 1798, Wellesley's military future was assured. He played a major role in successfully defeating the Indian allies of the French in a series of battles culminating in a brilliant but costly victory at Assaye in 1803, emerging as the leading 'Sepoy General' with the rank of Major-General. India developed Wellesley's hawkish eye for the importance of administrative logistical detail in difficult terrain, a characteristic that was to serve him well later in Spain.

His thirst for reputation continued to drive him. Successive victories against the French on the Spanish Peninsula from Vimiero in 1808 to Vittoria in 1812 followed by victories in the Pyrenees and the south of France earned him a formidable reputation and dukedom by 1814. Wellington's understated charisma and superb economic management of his armies in Spain coupled with an acute eye for timing and recognition of when precisely to strike placed him in a class of his own. Above all, he showed himself to be the consummate defensive tactician. He was now to do battle for the first time with the master of manoeuvre and attack.

Much has since been made of the similarities between the two opposing commanders at Waterloo, but on the eve of battle they were as academic as they are now. Both were born on islands in the same year, Napoleon on Corsica and Arthur Wellesley in Ireland. Both lost their fathers while young and both were educated in France. Ironically they were to share the same mistresses in Paris, were at ease with mathematics and the study of maps and topography. Hannibal was jointly admired and Ceaser's 'Commentaries' taken on campaign.

Wellington's pinnacle of success was, however, to prove Napoleon's nadir. It was the differences that set them apart. Wellington unlike Napoleon was at the top of his game – soon to be demonstrated at Waterloo – while Napoleon was past his prime. The coolly calculating Wellington was intellectually sharp enough to appreciate that Napoleon would be unpredictably dangerous, but was supremely confident he could deal with him. Despite the early dubious performance of the British army on land, directly experienced by Wellesley in Flanders in 1793, he was not

Wellington was at the height of his military prowess at Waterloo. [Wellington Museum]

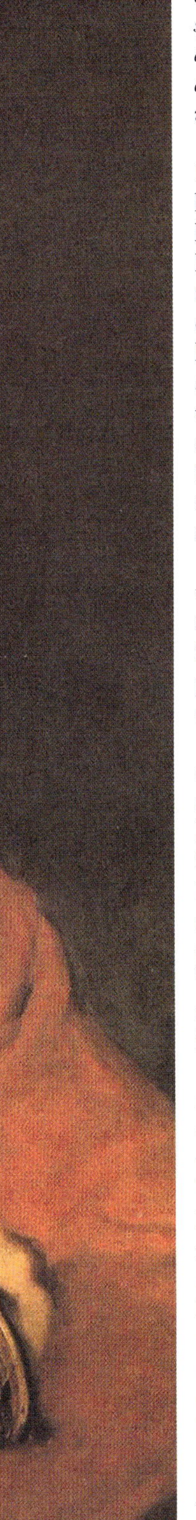

intimidated by the French, claiming in 1808 that:

'I am not afraid of them, as everybody else seems to be; and secondly, because if what I hear of the system of manoeuvre is true, I think it is a false one as against steady troops. I suspect all the continental armies were more than half-beaten before the battle was begun'.[6]

From Talevera on the Spanish Peninsula in 1809, Wellington was to demonstrably prove that his thin red line was the perfect foil for Napoleon's battering-ram approach with massed columns. Napoleon had respect for Wellington's victories in the difficult Peninsula, but considered him out of his own league in terms of military prowess. Wellington had fought 24 battles and sieges before Waterloo, and all but one, the siege of Burgos, had been victories. Napoleon had won 60 of his 70 battles and all of them of far greater scale. He had led armies of 200,000 men while concurrently acting as head of state. The forces about to close at Waterloo were only about this in total.

Napoleon projected *la Gloire de France,* whereas Wellington presented the image of a 'gentleman' player. Although this modest façade suggested the gifted amateur can always prevail, beneath the relaxed demeanor lurked a consummate professional.

Wellington even dressed like an amateur. The only concession to uniform at Waterloo was a low cocked hat adorned with the four cockades of Britain, Spain, Portugal and the Netherlands. Apart from this he wore comfortable civilian clothes. Lord Edward Somerset, commanding a brigade of the Household Cavalry remarked that Wellington passed him by at Waterloo as if *'riding for pleasure'.* This irreverent approach endeared him to his soldiers, not taken with too much finery, detecting in this a more practical professional.

Wellington's dullness of dress in fact marked him out on the battlefield, which was part of the intention, to inspire confidence. Napoleon was revered, even loved by his soldiers whereas Wellington held the unqualified respect of his. He had learned what not to do under the misguided management of the Duke of York in the Flanders campaign of 1793. Unfortunate lessons tend to be more enduring than those from success. When Sergeant William Wheeler, a Peninsula veteran with the 51st Regiment learned that Wellington rather than the inexperienced Prince of Orange would be leading them in Belgium he wrote in his diary:

'Our men were almost frantic, every soldier you met told you the joyful news… 'Glorious news. Nosey has got the command: won't we give them a drubbing now".[7]

'Wellington's thin red line was the perfect foil for Napoleon's battering-ram approach'

Wellington's taut, lithe and athletic demeanor physically demonstrated he was in his prime, unlike the flabby Napoleon, who was the same age. Wellington's physical stamina, gained from long years campaigning in Spain and Portugal was undiminished. There was no sallow skin, paunch, curtailment of riding or unintentional dozing during the day. He had less than three hours sleep during the night of the Duchess of Richmond's ball on 15/16th June after discovering that Napoleon had moved into Belgium. He directed operations from the saddle continuously until midnight the following day, riding from Brussels to Quatre-Bras, to Frasnes, to Ligny then back to Quatre-Bras and then on to Genappe covering 50 to 60 kilometres. His second day in the saddle on the 17th June after only another three hours sleep meant a further 20 kilometres and no sleep until midnight. On the day of the battle on the 18th Wellington was up at 03.00 and riding by 06.00 and would be in the saddle for the next 16 hours, directing an extremely close run battle, with all the physical shocks and emotional tensions that that entails. Many of his staff were killed around him. By the end of the battle Wellington had achieved maybe nine hours sleep out of 72, with at least 55 of these on horseback.

This understated strength was personified by a solitary nature, which added to his aura of competence. He was a disciplinarian, often stern with an outwardly cold and aloof manner and extremely sparing in his praise. Plans were always played close to his chest, which often caused complaints and umbrage among his staff and might occasionally reduce morale. He never felt any obligation to explain himself. When his second in command Lord Uxbridge mustered the courage to ask what the plan for Waterloo might be, Wellington responded: *'Bonaparte has not given me any idea of his projects; and as my plans will depend on his, how can you expect me t tell you what mine are?'*[5] Little blame could be attached to the surprise caused by Napoleon's skilful insertion of his own army between the two Allied armies because Wellington never publicly conjectured what might happen. He realised he was at a disadvantage at Waterloo, but characteristically never gave any sign of it. He simply awaited Napoleon's next move, having established himself in a strong defensive position, but knowing he was cut off from his Prussian allies.

Wellington, unlike Napoleon, rarely if ever delegated on the battlefield. As a consequence he was on the move all day, generally mounted, dashing from trouble spot to trouble spot with his staff trailing behind. Battlefield orders were given personally direct, or if

4. Napoleon and Soult, A. Roberts, Waterloo, P. xxxiv.
5. R Holmes, *Wellington. The Iron Duke*, BBC Wales Documentary, 2010
6. Wellington, A. Roberts, *Napoleon and Wellington*, P. 40.
7. Wheeler, *The Letters of Private Wheeler*, 29 May 1815, P. 161.

Blücher: Simple, but Competent in the Field

appropriate by staff officers. He would address anybody he needed to, from division commander to lowly soldier. Tight control was maintained. Quick decisions were made and orders issued at every stage of the battle. At Waterloo the Duke characteristically gave orders to those he considered the battle-winners: the infantry or artillery. He left Uxbridge to lead the cavalry.

Wellington was a brilliant defensive tactician and a proven master of profiting from his enemy's mistakes. He waited for Napoleon to display some. Despite being temporarily out manoeuvred, he continued to superbly manage his army economically. Wellington's personal demeanour radiated confidence and he could be positively lethal in the timing of his offensive counter-strokes. He waited on the dominant ridge, his Anglo-Allied force occupied and prepared to check-mate his opponent, should there be any mistakes in the opening moves. Wellington believed his pithy and pragmatic responses would far outweigh any 'fancy' schemes the French might throw at him. As he later explained in a conversation recorded by Sir William Fraser:

'They [the French] *planned their campaigns just as you might make a splendid piece of harness. It looks very well; and answers very well; until it gets broken; and then you are done for. Now I made my campaign of ropes. If anything went wrong, I tied a knot and went on'.*[8]

Blücher was a poor strategist, but an effective and practical leader on the Napoleonic battlefield. [Wellington Museum]

FIELD MARSHAL BLÜCHER

Field Marshal Gebhard von Blücher - old *Marshal Vorwarts* - was in command of the Prussian army, a soldier's soldier, brave, loyal and totally unimpressed by the numerous defeats inflicted already by Napoleon. His surfeit of occasionally misdirected energy was perfectly countered by the man he called 'the brains', his coolly calculating Chief of Staff, the Count von Gneisenau. Blücher's chief was no anglophile, but Wellington liked the bluff Field Marshal, whose pounding was far more effective than his manoeuvre. *'He was a very fine fellow'* declared Wellington, *'and where ever there was any question of fighting, always ready and eager – if anything too eager'.* The 77-year old Blucher had an addled mind, suffering from the mental delusion that he had been impregnated by an elephant. Despite this he was, re-instated as commander of the Prussian army again in 1815, his Army Chief of Staff General Gerhard von Scharnhorst writing he should lead *'though he has a hundred elephants inside him!'*[9]

Wellington would give orders to anyone who needed direction, from division commander to lowly soldier.

Napoleon (centre) with his cavalry chief Murat (left) on campaign. He was not to demonstrate his creative flair at Waterloo.

NAPOLEON BONAPARTE

Napoleon Bonaparte was 46 years old at Waterloo, the same age as the Duke of Wellington. He had been a soldier for 30 years, displaying a superior generalship that had enabled him to win all but 10 of the 72 battles he fought during his lifetime. His signature dress was an Imperial Guard cavalry uniform partially covered by a well-worn, shabby grey greatcoat. The Emperor preferred comfortable clothes, much to the despair of his tailor Bastide, who had to keep these outfits under repair, because he liked to wear them a long time. On his head was a battered half-moon shaped black hat, producing his instantly recognizable profile. Wellington admitted in 1814 at Paris that he

was glad he had never come across that distinctive silhouette in battle. *'I would at any time rather have heard that a reinforcement of 40,000 men had joined the French army'* he confided *'than that he had arrived to take command'*.

Wellington the master of practical tactical improvisation well appreciated Napoleon's shrewd battlefield opportunism. Nobody ever really knew what he would do next. Field Marshall Prince Karl Phillipp Wrede, who served with Napoleon between 1805 to 1813 asked Napoleon what was the secret theory behind his brilliant tactical and strategic successes. The response was typically enigmatic: *'Je n'en ai pas. Je n'ai point de plan de campagne'* (I don't have them. I don't have a campaign plan) he replied.' Napoleon simply aimed his blows whenever and wherever they would achieve maximum effect. He was completely unpredictable.[10]

Napoleon was born in 1769 into minor nobility in Corsica and received his 'gentleman' education within military schools and then learned his practical trade as a young artillery officer. Military success came first while commanding the artillery at the successful siege of royalist Toulon in 1793. This catapulted him into command of all artillery in the French Army of Italy and subsequently army commander. Its ragged, hungry and dispirited character was transformed into an effective fighting force that eventually defeated the Austrian and Piedmontese armies. Success in Egypt followed, dissipated by Nelson's British victory at the Nile in 1798. Napoleon returned to Europe and proclaimed himself First Consul and after a series of spectacular military and diplomatic successes, Emperor in 1804. His grip on Europe was consolidated by victory over Austria at Ulm and Austerlitz in 1805 and then over Prussia at Jena and Auerstadt in 1806.

One of the factors underpinning Napoleon's triumphs was an intuitive appreciation for the recent economic and industrial developments that made war on his vast scale so practically achievable. Improvements within the European road network aided the progress of his marching armies, whose size benefited from the increased productive capacity of the French arms industry. Napoleon's ability to raise such armies profited from his own administrative state reforms, and registration of France's rapidly expanding population, which reached 25.1 millions in 1780. Napoleon's mode of large scale warfare was profligate with lives. French writer and critic François René de Chateaubriand pointed out that with Napoleon no longer being Corsican and not quite French, he could afford to be *'lavish with French blood because he does not have a drop of it in his veins'.[11]*

Despite being extravagant with soldier's lives, Napoleon was always careful to cultivate their affection, which suggested they were worth something to him. Having risen through the ranks from a

8. Ibid, P. 534.
9. Wellington on Blücher, Longford P. 490, Scharnhorst, A Roberts, *Waterloo*, P. 24.
10. 8 Napoleon's Wrede quote, A Roberts, *Napoleon and Wellington*, P. 177.
11. De Chateaubriand quote, Ibid, P. 12.

Napoleon: The Master of Practical Improvisation

sous-lieutenant to emperor, he deliberately fostered a profound bond between himself and all ranks. He needed to love and understand his troops so they would reciprocate and do their best for him. Following the battle of Austerlitz in 1805 he adopted the children of some of his dead soldiers and had them educated. Napoleon deliberately promoted charisma and his soldiers loved him for it, following him to hell and enduring beyond, such as in Russia in 1812.

Napoleon was completely unpredictable, 'I don't have campaign plans'

Napoleon's strategic successes, however, inevitably led to a degree of tactical complacency. He commanded all the armies of France as well as being responsible for its political and civil affairs as head of state. Napoleon delegated through the chain of command and did not lead at the personal tactical level. At Waterloo his subordinate marshals sought flexibility to manoeuvre, precisely understanding how their various troop arms could be handled to best effect in changed weather or tactical conditions. Napoleon, who had virtually no practical experience of warfare at the regimental or company level, apart from putting down riots in revolutionary Paris, consistently overruled his lower tier commanders. He never commanded infantry in battle at the low level yet it was to be the superior firepower of opposing British infantry that was to be his nemesis at Waterloo.

This shortfall of practical soldierly judgement, long transcended by political or strategic imperatives, had already unhinged previous military successes by 1813. The long drawn out campaign in Spain and Portugal – the 'Spanish Ulcer' – proved a pointless military endeavour. Napoleon only visited Spain once, ejecting Sir John Moore's British Army at Coruna in 1809. Command thereafter was devolved to his Marshals, none of whom could contain the guerrilla war waged by the Spanish and a new British expeditionary force commanded by Wellington. Meanwhile the 1812 Russian campaign was a catastrophe: indecisive battles were fought at Smolensk and Borodino followed by a disastrous retreat through an unremitting winter from Moscow. Military mismanagement cost Napoleon two armies: one slowly in Spain, the other within months on the frozen

WAS NAPOLEON'S PERFORMANCE AT WATERLOO DOGGED BY ILL HEALTH?

Some historians have argued that Napoleon's medical condition contributed to the disastrous French outcome to the battle of Waterloo. As many as ten real or exaggerated medical problems have been cited for Napoleon's poor performance at Waterloo.

Napoleon's apparent torpor on the morning of the 17th June, when some poor key decisions were made, has been blamed on a condition called acromegaly. This can produce a form of listlessness and over-optimism. Other reported maladies include an inflammation of the bladder and urinary tract, originally identified at Borodino during the Russian campaign in 1812. During the night of the 16/17th June 1815 Napoleon was also diagnosed with collapsed haemorrhoids. This painful malady was treated by his surgeon Baron Larrey, bathing with warm water and applying leeches. By the following morning Napoleon was up and in the saddle. Like all battlefield soldiers the Emperor was exposed to the elements, variable diets and harsh physical conditions. These required a variety of treatments for constipation, cystitis and occasional exhaustion. Warfare was physically and mentally hard. But even after the inordinately harsh Russian winter campaign of 1812, Napoleon emerged with excellent health.

On the eve of Waterloo Napoleon was a 46-year old soldier past his physical prime.

Napoleon in his prime.

His enforced idleness at Elba contributed to a stout physique, which in itself is not necessarily incapacitating for a senior commander. Soldiers recognizing his distinctive profile at distance during the Waterloo campaign were shocked to see him close up. An officer who saw him at Ligny remarked:

'He had grown much stouter than when he was at Leipzig, and looked yellow. If it had not been for his grey coat and hat, I should hardly have recognized him. His cheeks were sunken and he looked much older'.

His health may well have deteriorated at Elba. Another officer commented on his appearance on return from exile:

'Napoleon's stoutness has increased rapidly. His head had become enlarged and more deeply set between his shoulders. His pot-belly was unusually pronounced for a man of forty-five. Furthermore, it was noticeable that during this campaign that he remained on horseback much less than in the past…his dull white complexion, his heavy walk made him appear very different'.

Nevertheless, this is the description of a man who had schemed his successful escape with the vanguard of an invading army from Elba; who accompanied them on the 800 kilometre march to Paris and attracted two divisions of troops to his colours en route. He was astute enough to negotiate his way around awkward obstacles and was industriously issuing imperial decrees within two weeks of arriving on the French mainland.

Napoleon lived a hard and 'fast' life and could subsist on the powerful adrenalin that fuelled his boundless ambition. He was driven 70 miles to Laon at dawn on 12th June just before the invasion of Belgium, worked all the next day before travelling to Beaumont on the border. On the 15th June he was on horseback for nearly 18 hours in sweltering heat, directing operations against the Prussians. Like many high ranking officers he tended to set up movements by night and snatch brief periods of sleep during the day, as his instructions were being executed. He was weary after being up all night during the invasion at Charleroi and in the saddle directing the battle of Ligny from early afternoon until nightfall, in the same summer heat. Pauses on the 17th were less about torpor, more complacence that Allied resistance had been broken and that Brussels was his for the taking. His traditional energy was visible to all riding with the French vanguard from Quatre-Bras to La Belle Alliance through the driving rain of a severe summer storm. If he was irritated by constipation, bladder or skin ailments, they do not appear to have effected his mental or physical performance. As one French officer was moved to comment on 15th June:

'Wellington was so far out-generalled; he was disconcerted by an offensive movement which he had not foreseen, and he had thus lost the whole plan of the campaign'.

Napoleon's physical condition was what one might expect from an over-weight senior officer past his physical prime. No French contemporary eye-witnesses are commenting that Napoleon's military performance was in any way below par. This was a man in his usual health subjected to the normal physical rigours of war but displaying the sort of energy that would dismay commanders with less determination.

There were moments when he was obliged to rest, but no lack of resolve throughout the battle that was to follow at Waterloo. Indeed there is evidence of great rallying power after formidable exertion. Wellington, who was more athletic and equally energised, admits his victory was *'a close run thing'.*

Napoleon's health was not therefore a key factor in explaining his defeat. He was to live a further six years on Saint-Helena after the battle of Waterloo. Recent medical research suggests he finally succumbed to stomach cancer rather than arsenic poisoning or over-zealous medical treatments. None of the ailments mentioned at Waterloo appear to have recurred in exile.

A less flattering image by Girodet de Roucy in 1812. Napoleon was past his physical prime by the time of Waterloo, but in cerebral terms he was as formidable as ever. [Musee de Chateauroux]

Russian steppes. A resurgence of tactical flair occurred during the final battles in France in 1813 and 1814 but was overcome by Allied doggedness. It was too late and Napoleon was forced to abdicate.

Napoleon quickly demonstrated in early 1815 that he had not lost his strategic foresight or ability to quickly deploy his corps across good road networks to appear where least expected. He worsted the British and Prussians at Quatre-Bras and Ligny by swiftly positioning his armies in between, precisely where he wanted them. He could astutely set up the chess board for conflict, but was losing the flair required for lethal 'check' moves. These were delegated to his Marshals who were by now unfortunate choices. The good Marshals were missing on return from exile. Many were in the wrong posts, over promoted or creatively spent, or like the hapless Marshal Ney, suffering from battle fatigue.

Napoleon felt artillery was his battle-winning arm. As an artilleryman he had massed his batteries to full effect at Wagram in 1809, Borodino in 1812 and seriously mauled the Prussians at Ligny. He was well used to achieving local superiority by opportunistic campaign moves, but less knowledgeable about how his Imperial Guard might take a particular objective. This was the stuff of subordinates.

'They are brave fellows, those English troops of yours' he commented to Whig MP John Fazakerley, visiting at St Helena after Waterloo. *'They are worth more than the others. Next to them, I consider the Prussians the best'.*[10] Yet Napoleon seriously underestimated both. He considered his own judgement superior to that of his Marshals and was always ready to override them; but their recent experience, particularly against the British in the Peninsula was more relevant than his own. Napoleon had never faced commanders who hid their primary units behind dead ground. Neither had he appreciated the ability of the British to hold ground in the face of severe punishment and still mete out swinging retribution with disciplined infantry firepower.

Napoleon past his best was about to encounter an opposing commander at the pinnacle of his.

---

11. Napoleon's quote, Ibid, P. 155.

'There, it all depends on that article, whether we do the business or not'

WELLINGTON'S 'INFAMOUS' ARMY

Whig politician Thomas Creavy asked Wellington how he expected to fare in the coming battle on the eve of Waterloo. Wellington responded by pointing out a British soldier wandering through a Brussels park. *'There, it all depends on that article, whether we do the business or not'* he said. *'Give me enough of it, and I am sure'.*[12]

Wellington did not have enough. Only 25 of his 84 infantry battalions were British and just 36% of the army. For every one of 'that article' there were two Germans, Dutch or Belgians. There were seven nationalities in all and eight including the Prussians. Wellington had asked his War Office for 40,000 infantry, 15,000 cavalry, 150 guns and a staff of his own choosing. He received only 30,000 and a four page apology from the Duke of York, the British Commander-in-Chief. Until Napoleon invaded Belgium, Britain was neither at war or peace, so the militia could not be called out to support the regulars. Many of his veteran Peninsula War troops were in America. *I have got an infamous army, very weak and ill equipped and a very inexperienced staff'* declared a clearly irritated Wellington. There were four infantrymen to every one cavalryman.[13]

Wellington's soldiers were hastily assembled. Few of them, after 22 years of Revolutionary and Napoleonic wars that ended with Napoleon's abdication in 1814, thought they would ever be called upon to fight again. Captain Verner with the 7th Hussars had been policing 'No Corn Bill' riots in London when it was reported Napoleon had escaped Elba. *No more was heard upon the* [Corn Law] *subject than if panic never existed'* he recalled. Within 12 hours his regiment was marching to Brighton to embark for Flanders. Militia men supplemented regular battalions and Wellington mixed lesser experienced units with veteran. Others like Sergeant Thomas Morris with the 73rd Regiment already in theatre, despite being billeted with a miller with two pretty daughters was *'tired of the monotony'.*

Standing firm in line throughout the day despite visceral casualties was the lot of Wellington's infantry. The 27th Inniskillings died virtually to a man in square at Waterloo. [NAM].

Private soldier 44th (East Essex) Regiment. British soldiers only made up one third of Wellington's 'infamous army'

All waiting units prior to Napoleon's invasion of Belgium shared the 'restlessness' of the 73rd *'and an anxiety to know what the French were about, and how soon our services would be required'.* The moment had arrived.[14]

They faced battle alongside a lot of foreigners whom they either disdained or mistrusted. The eight battalions of the King's German Legion were an exception. They were a crack unit loyal to George III

Smoke and the appalling noise often resulted in fumbling the reloading process. The British line. [Re-enactment]

and were accepted as the equal of any British unit. The others were much less so. The Heterogeneous contingents had little in common, neither language, nor customs or ideals. Hanoverian field battalions had some experience but newly raised Landwehr militia units had none. They were the largest contingent after the British. Five days before Waterloo Wellington received a request for powder and cartridges to exercise the Hanoverian Brigade Reserve at Ath in the Netherlands, because *'many soldiers have never fired a shot'*.

The Protestant Dutch at 13% of the whole were an uneasy mix with the 6% Catholic Belgians. Both states had been under French control throughout most of the Revolutionary and Napoleonic wars. The Dutch kingdom was formed just 12 months before, rankling the Belgians who aspired to independence. Both dressed in uniforms almost exactly like the French and were commanded by officers who had recently fought for France. Small wonder they were regarded with scepticism by the British soldiers. The Brunswickers and Nassauers formed 8% and 10% of the force respectively and were largely newly recruited and inexperienced 18-year olds. The British formed only a third of an army of which 45% spoke German as their common language.

They awaited reinforcement from a 130,000 strong Prussian army, reduced somewhat after Ligny 48 hours before. Despite inexperience, Prussian field units were well trained and the majority were tough and fired up with resurgent nationalism. Nearly half were Landwehr or militia. They were itching to close with the French after years of humiliating occupation. The French reciprocated the bitterness. Unlike the rest of the Allies they were either marching or attacking the entire day. Much of their fighting was not in open lines and columns but street fighting within the narrow streets, and alleys of Plancenoit village. They brawled their way through gardens, houses and churchyards as individuals and small groups. The French were shot at less than five metres away and every house and room had to be cleared with bayonet and musket butt. Von Bülow's IV Corps were totally unused to this type of close-in no-holds fighting, having missed Ligny. The Prussians were to perform better than expected.

Wellington's troops were required mainly to defend, an easier and less vulnerable option. Two fundamental skills were needed to do this well during the Napoleonic era: proficient musketry and foot drill. British soldiers were armed with the India pattern 'Brown Bess' musket and the foreign contingents had a like weapon. British Light Infantry and the King's German Legion had the more superior rifled Baker rifle.

A soldier aiming and firing his musket at an enemy over 100 metres away in a battle situation was going to knock him down on average once, in every 30 shots. If the range was reduced to 50 to 70 metres the hit rate rose dramatically to one in three, whereas volley fire below 50 metres was usually devastating.[15] Proficiency at loading and firing was therefore key; anything less than two to three shots per minute was considered poor. The complex procedure had to be hurriedly achieved amid a virtual storm of cannon-shot, grape and opposing musket fire. Smoke and the appalling noise assailed the senses and distracted immature soldiers into fumbling the process. They had arrived on the battlefield soaking wet and tired having marched and counter-marched for three days from their cantonment areas to Brussels. Many had fought a bloody battle at Quatre-Bras already and then retreated through the driving rain of a violent summer storm. Smoke and the undulating ground at Waterloo restricted visibility and orders were transmitted amid the dreadful noise by drum, bugle or shouted command. Confusion about what was going on and disorientation would have been the norm.

Standing firm on the Mont Saint-Jean ridgeline and enduring howling shot and shell proved grim work. The impacts of bouncing cannon balls were so frequent and the effect on the human torso so catastrophic that apprehension bordering on terror was the lot of survivors convinced they had only temporarily been spared. Although the drill manual directed three ranks, in practice the British stood in two. More ground could be covered. There was also less chance of the third rank accidentally shooting those forward under pressure. The aim was to bring as many weapons as possible to bear on an approaching column or line and not to fire volleys in excess of 100 metres, then quickly reload to get a further shot off at a closing enemy.

Coordinated drill movements were required to present these lines tactically where they were required. The colours were in the centre and officers stood behind the second rank. At 75 paces per minute 100 metres might be covered enabling a British battalion to level 550 muskets. The outcome was normally decided at about this distance; artillery killed more men up to 100 metres. After that the line might surge forward to close with the bayonet. This had a triangular sectioned 15 to 17 inches long blade that fitted into a cylindrical socket at the end of the musket barrel. Its effectiveness was more psychological than physical.

It was essential not to get caught in line by cavalry. Forming square required timely decision, cool heads and good training to be successful in the face of onrushing cavalry. Failure was punished severely. A 69th Regiment square was cut to pieces at Quatre-Bras, having left the decision to form from extended line too late, as also a King's German Legion battalion near La Haye Sainte. Squares were especially vulnerable to artillery and skirmisher fire; 66% of the 27th Inniskilling Regiment were to fall in square at Waterloo.

Standing firmly in line, wet and tired from the start, unable to see through the smoke and enduring visceral casualties from flying missiles was the lot of most of Wellington's infantry. Group solidarity and individual leadership held them together in a battle of attrition. The common experience was that of infantry lines firing en-masse point blank into each other. Just over 17,000 of Wellington's men fell at Waterloo. Thirty percent of his officers became casualties and 17 soldiers fell alongside each officer. Even by the brutal standards of the day, the battle of Waterloo was exceptionally violent.

12. Creavy, A Roberts, Waterloo, P. 23.

13. Figures, M Adkin, The Waterloo Companion, P. 37. Wellington, E Longford, Wellington: The Years of the Sword, P. 484-5.

14. Verner, Reminiscences of William Verner 7th Hussars, Society for Historical Research 1965, P. 39. Morris, ed J Selby, Thomas Morris, P. 66.

15. Musketry figures, Adkin, P. 165-6.

'Animated with the most inflexible courage and ardent enthusiasm towards the Emperor Napoleon'

THE FRENCH

Infantry quality was the deciding factor at Waterloo, only they could take or hold ground. Napoleon commanded a first-rate fighting formation of 123,000 largely veterans with 246 guns. The Armée du Nord was nationally cohesive, unlike Wellington's force and Bonapartist virtually to a man. The Bourbons had been unpopular, controlling the highest positions in church and state. Petty injustices had been meted out on what was left of the army that had escaped peace-time disbandment when Napoleon went into exile. It had fiercely resented its toppling from favour.

French grenadier infantryman. The majority of Napoleon's army were veterans.

Most units were therefore recently reformed from previous cadres and re-equipped. *'The battalions were filled up with restored prisoners; with pensionaries and with new levies'* recalled an officer during the hectic build-up. *'Arms of all kinds, artillery of all calibre, and equipages innumerable, seemed to issue as if by magic from the arsenals and foundries; and within a few days France was transformed into a vast camp'.*

The average French soldier was a veteran; many of the eighteen year olds had likely fought in the final campaigns of 1813-14. According to one officer they were *'animated with the most inflexible courage and the most ardent enthusiasm towards their former leader, the Emperor Napoleon'.* Hatred of the foreign invader emotionally bound them together. Invading Belgium had been met with universal approval, especially the restoration of their right to loot. *'French soldiers treated the farmers and peasantry with the most extreme rigour'* recalled one of their officers, *'considering pillage as one of their most indisputable rights'.*

Napoleon's *modus operandi* was built around his proven ability to move quickly and decisively with his all-arms balanced corps that contained infantry, cavalry and integral artillery. March discipline, often distracted by their propensity to plunder was poor, but they nevertheless made the best use of roads and locally foraged provisions. These corps could move quickly then unite to fight and had unexpectedly materialised between Wellington and Blücher's armies.

There were over three infantrymen to every cavalryman in the six corps of the Armée du Nord; each infantry battalion averaged 520 all-ranks with 460 troopers or hussars in cavalry regiments. Despite the combined all-arms nature of the corps the constituent parts did not always work well together. An officer described the *'implacable hatred'* that existed between some corps, with virtual *'open war'* where there was *'no reciprocal confidence, no common feeling, but everywhere selfishness, arrogance and rapacity'.* The Imperial Guard, which creamed off the best of the veterans, regarded itself as an elite private army whose arrogance was much resented by the others. Units could even come to blows over disputed foraging rights, whereas the Guard had its own unique logistics wagon train.[16]

Ironically French soldiers distrusted their officers as much as they revered Napoleon. Suspicions of Bourbon treachery lay at the core of these implicit divisions. Isolation at Elba had desensitised Napoleon from the betrayal neurosis that afflicted much of the army and this had an effect on the passage of command information. The Armée du Nord was to repeatedly wrong-foot itself through staff misinterpretations of key orders during the battle.

At Waterloo the French role was to primarily attack, which made them more exposed. But as veteran formations they were well versed and drilled to do this. Only 15 of 103 infantry battalions would be deployed in defence and these to stop the advancing Prussians at Plancenoit.

For most of the day French soldiers were advancing into the teeth of Allied cannon and musket fire in battalion columns, which were companies in three ranks on a two company frontage or in division size battalion columns. The men marched forward at about 75 paces a minute tightly bunched in three rank company lines one after the other virtually treading on the heels of the battalion only 5 metres ahead. Such formations were clumsy and difficult to hold in formation while ploughing through muddy valley bottoms and scaling slippery slopes. They were exceptionally vulnerable to artillery fire and cavalry attacks. Just the front three ranks could see with peripheral vision on the flanks. Only objectives on higher ground could be made out from the ranks through the smoke. The battle was felt rather than seen. Howling artillery strikes would suddenly sweep away a dozen or more men in the ranks in a welter of screams and flying limbs before the ranks closed and they would proceed. It was a virtual herd mentality. Instruction was heard by drum, bugle and shouted word, barely distinguishable in the maelstrom of noise that accompanied incoming fire.

Ahead of these advancing compact columns were swarms of *voltigeurs* or light infantry skirmishers. These sharpshooters moved forward in rushes, before pausing and engaging the enemy ahead with deliberate aimed shots. They were especially troublesome to formed squares, which offered a huge target.

The first shot in battle fired by the Frenchman with his IX Charleville musket was likely to be his most accurate. Loading was rushed with increasing technical problems arising from misfires and jamming becoming more pronounced at each shot. 'Hang Fire' from the third rank was especially dangerous. They could literally get away with murder by disposing of disliked or suspect leaders in the forward ranks. An earlier 1791 regulation specified the third rank should pass forward reloaded muskets, but nobody was prepared to pass across his weapon in the heat of battle. One French source suggests that perhaps as many as a quarter of French infantry casualties may have been self-inflicted by the third rank. Manoeuvring into square to receive a cavalry charge from column

Such was the press during the French cavalry attacks that riders in the centre were lifted bodily from the ground.

formation was exceptionally difficult. When the British heavy cavalry brigades struck D'Erlon's mass infantry column attacks during the early afternoon, the flanks and front of the formations imploded and broke into a rout.[17]

The mass attacks by 34 regiments of French cavalry were an equally sorry experience. So constrained was the area of attack that the centre rank horsemen were occasionally lifted bodily from the ground by the pressure of the outer ranks closing into the centre where they had been funnelled by the fire from the two flanking farm complexes at Hougoumont and La Haye Sainte, to their left and right. The cavalry advance was possibly set in mass motion accidentally by a ripple effect of units galloping off after the others anxious not to dissipate the momentum of the attack following unclear orders. It resulted in uncoordinated mayhem beyond the Mont Saint-Jean ridgeline when it was discovered, that far from retreating, the Allies were securely ensconced within infantry squares. No horse will willingly gallop into a mass of fire fenced off by a phalanx of bayonets so the French cavalry had no recourse except to dash themselves against the squares or vainly gallop in between, picked off by volleys of converging cross-fire from differently angled squares.

The lot of the French attackers was to expose themselves to shot and shell the entire day, advancing in easily targeted and vulnerable infantry columns, or ride across broken ground en masse easy prey to artillery and concentrated infantry fire from squares. By the end of the day the dead were heaped up to four high across the Mont St Jean ridgeline. French losses are debateable. It is impossible to differentiate between the defeat and subsequent rout. They may have totalled some 31,000 representing 40% of the whole. The Imperial Guard lost some 62% of its strength and losses of 55% are reported from one of the Reserve Cavalry Corps. By any measure, the day was a catastrophic experience for the average French fighting man.[18]

There was concern in the French line during the confusion of battle that casualties might be accidentally inflicted by the third rank on those in front. [re-enactment]

16. Officers, Anon, The Journal of the Three Days of Waterloo, P. 20-5.
17. Casualty claim, Adkin, P. 191 and 193.
18. Casualties, Adkin P.73 supplemented by S Bowden, Armies at Waterloo.

Walking
Wellington's Line at Waterloo

THE WATERLOO BATTLEFIELD TOUR

There are a number of good hotels local to Waterloo but many prefer to stay at Brussels 12 miles to the north. The quickest approach to the battlefield site is the Brussels RO ring road leaving at Exit 21 for Genappe-Braine-l'Alleud then coming off at Exit 23 for the Waterloo Centre. Another alternative is to drive south along the N5. A new battle museum also opened in 2015 - well worth a visit.

The N5 goes through the town of Waterloo, which was a small village at the time of the battle. Wellington spent the night before at the Inn in the centre of town opposite the original Royal Chapel. His headquarters has been converted to a museum with many interesting artefacts. On the same road, three miles beyond La Belle Alliance to the south is Napoleon's headquarters at Le Caillou, where he spent the night before Waterloo. It has also been converted to a museum.

Wellington's HQ in Waterloo

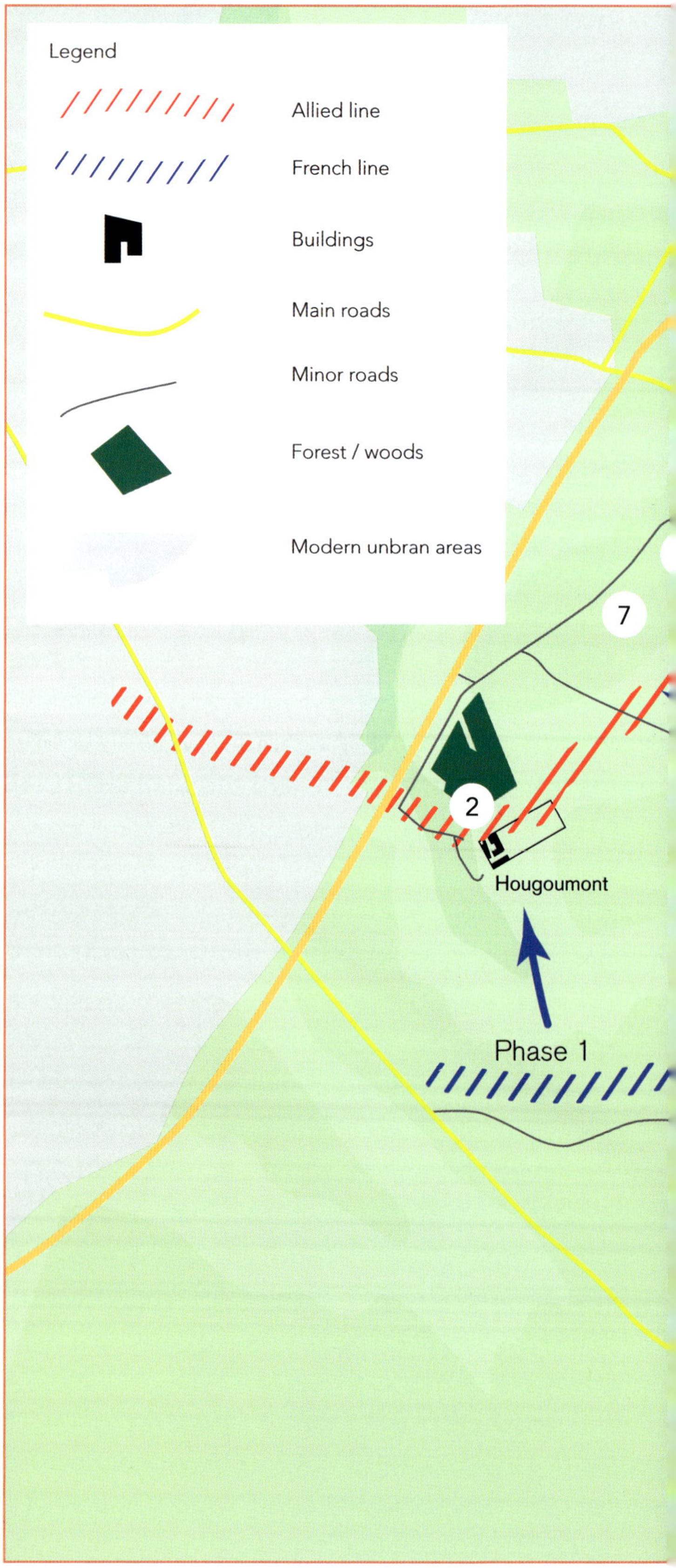

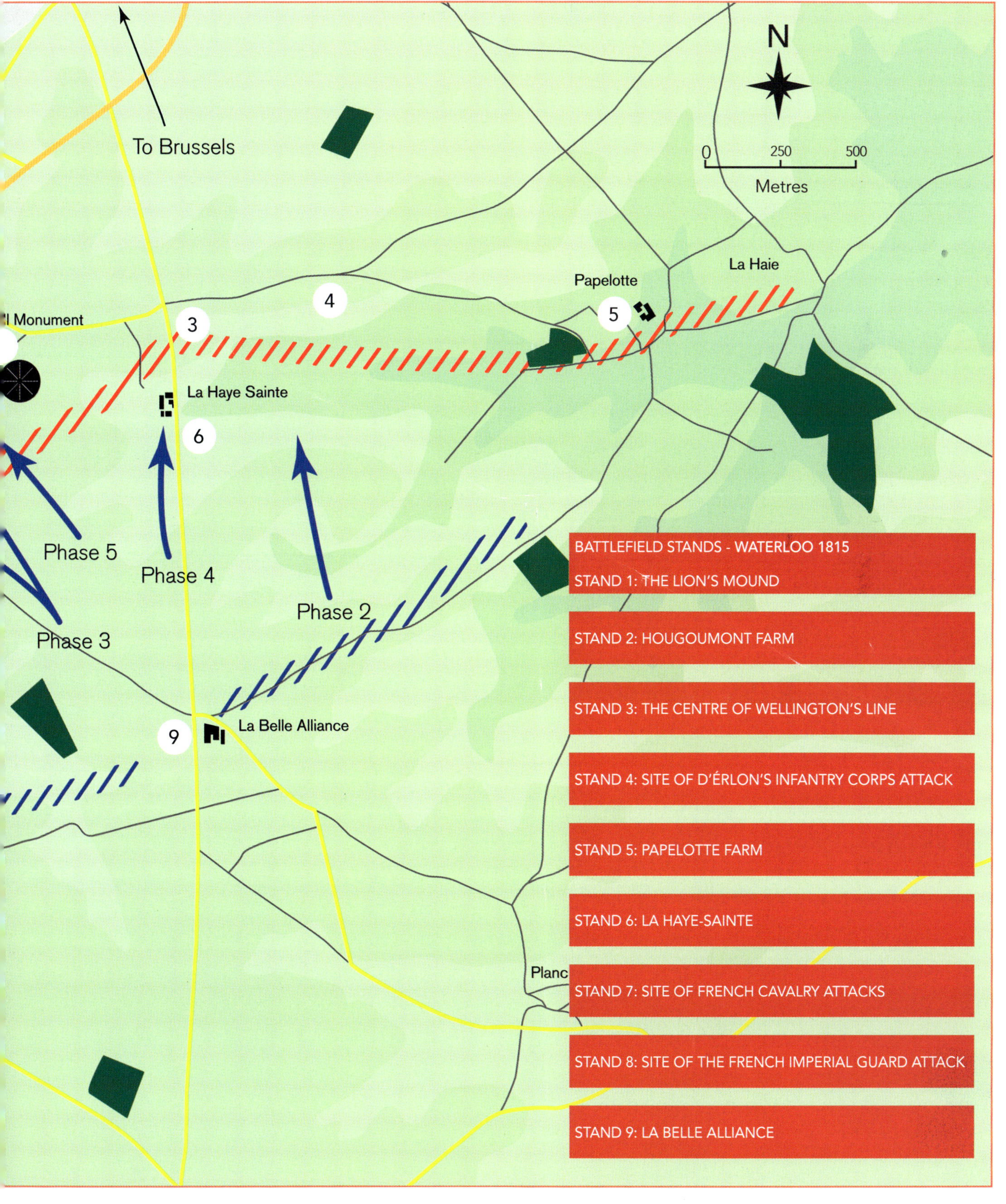
To Brussels
N
0   250   500
Metres
I Monument
4
3
Papelotte
La Haie
5
La Haye Sainte
6
Phase 5
Phase 4
Phase 3
Phase 2
La Belle Alliance
9
Planc
BATTLEFIELD STANDS - WATERLOO 1815
STAND 1: THE LION'S MOUND
STAND 2: HOUGOUMONT FARM
STAND 3: THE CENTRE OF WELLINGTON'S LINE
STAND 4: SITE OF D'ÉRLON'S INFANTRY CORPS ATTACK
STAND 5: PAPELOTTE FARM
STAND 6: LA HAYE-SAINTE
STAND 7: SITE OF FRENCH CAVALRY ATTACKS
STAND 8: SITE OF THE FRENCH IMPERIAL GUARD ATTACK
STAND 9: LA BELLE ALLIANCE

Napoleon's HQ at Le Caillou.

The Lion's Mound

THE LION'S MOUND

The Lion's mound is an artificial hill erected in the 1820s and is a good start point for a walking tour, with a car park alongside. It marks the spot where Prince William of Orange, one of Wellington's corps commanders, and heir to the Dutch throne, was wounded on the evening of the battle. The mound gives a spectacular 135-feet high view of the battlefield, which protected by Belgian law, has remained largely unchanged. All the main phases of the battle are easily observed from this point.

Hououmont, where the battle started is visible 1,200 yards to the south west. La Haye-Sainte, which D'Érlon's French infantry corps attacked is just 500 yards away to the south-east. The full extent of Wellington's line can be seen beyond, ending at Papelotte Farm, 1,600 yards to the east. Plancenoit village, where the Prussians eventually appeared is 2,800 yards to the south east and the white inn building at La Belle Alliance, Napoleon's vantage point and where Wellington met Blücher at the end of the battle is to its right, due south along the Brussels road 1,300 yards away. The area in front of the mound between La Haye-Sainte to the left and Hougoumont to the right saw the French massed cavalry attacks and the final attack of Napoleon's Imperial Guard. The view emphasises the small five square mile limited extent of the battlefield.

The view from the top of the Lion's Mound showing the crossroads and the left of Wellington's line beyond the car park, to the right is the farm at La Haye-Sainte.

The south gate at Hougoumont Farm successfully held by the Coldstream Guards.

HOUGOUMONT FARM

Walk the tarmac track south west from the Lion's Mound to the farm complex at Hougoumont. The buildings were under attack all day by some 15,000 French troops from Reille's II Corps. It was defended by the light companies of all three Foot Guards regiments and two battalions from the 2nd Guards Brigade, who bore the brunt of the fighting as well as Nassauers, Hanoverians and King's German Legion soldiers. Despite being set on fire and penetrated at one point, the complex never fell.

Private Mathew Clay with the 2nd Battalion 3rd Foot Guards pictured the scene after a French penetration led by an axe-swinging officer got inside the gate at the height of the battle:

'On entering the courtyard I saw the doors or rather gates were riddled with shot holes, and it was also very wet and dirty; in its entrance lay many dead bodies of the enemy; one I particularly noticed which appeared to have been a French officer, but they were scarcely distinguishable, being to all appearances as though they had been very much trodden upon, and covered with mud'.

The garrison had just killed all the French troops that had forced their way through the main gate.

'I saw Lieutenant Colonel MacDonnell [in command] carrying a large piece of wood or trunk of a tree in his arms, (one of his cheeks marked with blood, his charger lay bleeding within a short distance) with which he was hastening to secure the gates against the renewed attack of the enemy, which was most vigorously repulsed'.

The significance for the defence of the bastions held at Hougoumont and La Haye-Sainte was that they broke up the scale

'The conflict' according to Private Mathew Clay was 'bloody, desperate and unyielding'. [Re-enactment]

and momentum of the French attacks. An anonymous French officer in Reille's Corps described:

'The enemy had strengthened their positions with great art; they had made loopholes in the walls of the buildings, and thence fired upon us with great advantage. The battle upon this point became gradually most desperate, each side reinforcing its party. Some of our battalions and squadrons, making a detour round the angles of the position, lanced themselves upon the masses in its rear. The enemy, seeing this attack reinforced their columns, whilst our generals did the same. The conflict was accordingly bloody, desperate and unyielding'.[19]

19. Clay, ed G Glover, A Narrative of the Battles of Quatre-Bras and Waterloo; with the Defence of Hougoumont, P. 26. French Officer, The Journal of the Three Days of the Battle of Waterloo, Anon, P. 45.

3 THE CENTRE OF WELLINGTON'S LINE

Left: The present day memorial to the men of the 27th Inniskilling Regiment, near the crossroads.

The cross roads, the centre of Wellington's line, which were sunken roads at the time. A solitary Elm tree stood to the right, where there is now a clump of trees

Walk past the Lion's Mound and proceed due east to the traffic lights at the cross roads. This was the centre of Wellington's line and his headquarters location when not on the move, distinguishable by a solitary elm tree. At the time the roads were sunken and unpaved and lined with holly bushes. Every fold of the battlefield is visible from this location, (left of the crossroads and looking south in the direction of La Belle Alliance). Wellington constantly moved up and down the line and frequently paused here. What was he thinking? Whig politician Thomas Creevey spoke to him immediately after the battle, when he was still animated by what had happened:

'It has been a damned serious business' he said. *'Blücher and I have lost 30,000 men. It has been the damned nice thing – the nearest run thing you ever saw in your life. Blücher lost 14,000 on Friday night, and got so damnably licked I could not find him on Saturday morning; so I was obliged to fall back to keep up my communications with him…'* He repeated so often its being *'so nice a thing – so nearly run a thing…By God! I don't think it would have been done if I had not been there'*.

Just behind the crossroads was where the 27th Regiment the Inniskillings died virtually to a man in square, nearly seven in ten fell. There is a stone nearby to commemorate the event. They stood in square because of the French cavalry attacks, presenting a fat target for the sharp-shooting French skirmishers and cannon around La Haye Sainte farm (directly ahead), after it was captured by the French. Captain John Kincaid with the 95th Rifles recalled:

'I shall never forget the scene which the field of battle presented about seven in the evening. I felt weary and worn out, less from fatigue than anxiety. Our division, which had stood upwards of 5,000 men at the commencement of the battle, had gradually dwindled down into a solitary line of skirmishers. The 27th Regiment were lying literally dead, in square, a few yards behind us…I had never yet heard of a battle in which everybody was killed; but this seemed likely to be an exception, as all were going by turns…Sir John Lambert continued to stand as our support, [behind them] at the head of three good old regiments, one dead (the 27th) and two living ones'.[20]

The 27th Regiment literally died in square. [Re-enactment]

The British infantry view of the approach of D'Érlon's infantry corps against the left of Wellington's line as seen from the Mont St Jean ridge, looking half right towards La Haye Sainte

4 SITE OF D'ÉRLON'S INFANTRY CORPS ATTACK

At about 200 yards beyond the crossroads, along the same road moving east, was the site of D'Érlon's massive infantry assault against the Mont Saint-Jean crest line. The French columns came in from the low ground to the right. With them was Captain Duthilt of the 45th Line Regiment, toiling up the muddy slope:

'The distance involved was not too great, and an average person on foot would have taken no more than five or six minutes to cover the ground; but the soft and rain-sodden earth and the tall rye slowed up our progress appreciably. As a result the English gunners had plenty of time in which to work destruction upon us.

'The charge was beaten, our pace quickened, and to repeated shouts of "Vive l'Empereur!" we rushed at the batteries. Suddenly our path was blocked; English battalions, concealed in a hollow road, stood up and fired at us at close range'.

They had brushed aside Bijlandt's Dutch-Belgian troops and opened an inviting 250 metre gap in the Allied line. This was promptly filled by Picton's 5th British Division and a further totally unexpected development. Captain Duthilt was so engrossed sorting out the confusion that the shattering volleys of Picton's men inflicted that he missed what happened next:

'Just as I was pushing one of our men back into the ranks I saw him fall at my feet from a sabre slash. I turned round instantly – to see English cavalry forcing their way into our midst and hacking us to pieces'.

Emerging from the low ground behind the Mont Saint-Jean ridgeline came two brigades of British heavy cavalry. More than 2,600 horsemen streamed across the sunken road in this area. D'Érlon's infantry

'Rain sodden earth and the tall rye slowed up our progress appreciably'

corps was put to flight, running back down the slope to the south. Galloping after them with the Scot's Greys was Corporal Dickinson, who recalled:

'I felt a strange thrill run through me, and I am sure my noble beast felt the same, for, after rearing for a moment, she sprang forward, uttering loud neighings and snortings, and leapt over the holly hedge at terrific speed. It was a grand sight to see the long line of giant grey horses dashing along with flowing manes and heads down, tearing up the turf about them as they went…

'Some of the wounded were firing at us as we passed; and poor Kinchant, who had spared one of these rascals, was himself shot by the officer he had spared. As we were sweeping down a steep slope on the top of them, they had to give way. Then those in front began to cry out for "quarter", throwing down their muskets and taking off their belts'. [21]

20. Wellington. Ed A Brett-James, The Hundred Days, P. 183-4. Kincaid, The Adventures in the Rifle Brigade, P. 170.

21. Duthilt, Brett-James, P. 115. Dickinson, ed F Llewellyn, Waterloo Recollections, P. 194 and 196.

⑤ PAPELOTTE FARM

This is the left of Wellington's line and is reached by continuing along the cobbled road that veers south east to the slopes of Papelotte farm. It was held by a brigade of Nassau infantry. The French captured some of the farm buildings and there was a friendly fire incident when the Prussians from von Ziethen's corps emerged from the east. Major von Neumann with the 2nd Brandenberg Regiment recalled:

'I was to throw out the French who had just occupied Smohain village [opposite Papelotte farm] after the Nassau infantry had fallen back…the Schützen and the Fusilier battalion advanced against the enemy skirmishers who fought back ferociously. This struggle continued until the enemy's general withdrawal began when our cavalry followed up'.

Henri Nieman with the 6th Uhlan Prussian cavalry paused at this point at nine o'clock that night and saw:

'The battlefield was almost cleared of the French army. It was an evening no pen is able to picture: the surrounding villages yet in flames, the lamentations of the wounded of both armies, the singing for joy; no one is able to describe nor find a name to give to those horrible scenes'.[22]

'No one is able to describe nor find a name to give to those horrible scenes'

The entrance to Papelotte Farm today

Prussian infantry repel a French attack. [Re-enactment]

6 LA HAYE-SAINTE

Return to position three at the traffic lights and turn left along the cycle route alongside the left of the road 300 yards to La Haye-Sainte farm. This was the second fortified farm, forward of Wellington's line that did so much to break up incoming French attacks. D'Erlon's infantry had to veer east of it while the French cavalry attacks were fired at on their right flank. It was held throughout the afternoon by the 2nd Light Battalion of the King's German Legion, crack troops armed with the Baker rifle. They held on until six o'clock when they ran out of ammunition and were wiped out by the French amid the blazing buildings.

The French battled their way inside the farm buildings. [Re-enactment]

Major George Baring defending with the King's German Legion recalled:

'What must have been my feelings therefore, when, on counting the cartridges, I found that, on average, there was not more than from three to four each!... On my exhortations to courage and economy of the ammunition, I received one unanimous reply: "No man will desert you – we will fight with you!" No pen, not even that of one who has experienced such moments, can describe the feeling which this excited in me; nothing can be compared with it!

'...the enemy, who soon observed our wants now boldly broke one of the doors; however, as only a few could come in at a time, these were instantly bayoneted, and the rear hesitated to follow. They now mounted the roof and walls, from which my unfortunate men were certain marks; at the same time they pressed in through the open barn, which could no longer be defended'.

They retreated into the garden. Lieutenant George Graeme an officer in the Hanoverian service, described the close quarter fighting that broke out as the French flocked through the farm buildings, pushing the survivors into the garden at the northern end of the complex:

'Some of the wounded soldiers of ours who lay there and cried out "pardon" were shot, the monsters saying, "Take that for the fine defence you have made".

'An officer and four men came in first; the officer got me by the collar, and said to his men, "C'est ce coquin". Immediately the fellows had their bayonets down, and made a dead stick at me, which I parried with my sword, the officer always running about and then coming to me again and shaking me by the collar; but they all looked so frightened and pale as ashes, I thought, "You shan't keep me", and I bolted through the lobby; they fired two shots after me, and cried out "Coquin", but did not follow me'.[23]

The present-day farm at La Haye-Sainte

22. Neumann, P Hofschröer, 1815. The Waterloo Campaign, P. 139. Nieman, A Uffindell and M Corum, Waterloo, Battleground Napoleon series, P. 76.
23. Baring, Brett-James, P. 143-4. Graeme, Ibid, P. 146.

7 SITE OF FRENCH CAVALRY ATTACKS

This is one of the best preserved sites of all, viewed from the narrow lane west of the Lion's Mound. The scene was watched with astonishment by the Allies, because the French attacked with cavalry alone. More than ten massive cavalry charges dashed uselessly among Wellington's infantry, standing secure in square. After each attack the French artillery opened fire again, causing terrible damage in the tight formations. This was the Allied low point during the battle, having to endure attacks for an hour and a half until about 5.30 pm. Captain Cavalié Mercer, commanding a troop of light horse artillery, watched them come:

'On they came in compact squadrons, one behind the other, so numerous that those of the rear were still below the brow when the head of the column was but at some 60 or 70 yards from our guns. Their pace was a slow but steady trot. None of your furious galloping charges was this, but a deliberate advance, at a deliberate pace, as of men resolved to carry their point. They moved in profound silence, and the only sound that could be heard from them amidst the incessant roar of battle was the low thunder-like reverberation of the ground beneath the simultaneous tread of so many horses…

I allowed them to advance unmolested until the head of the column might have been about 50 or 60 yards from us, and then gave the word "Fire!" The effect was terrible. Nearly the whole leading rank fell at

The area of the French cavalry attacks viewed from the Lion's Mound. The road marked the crest line for Wellington's right and behind it, the infantry formed in squares. The cavalry attacked over the open ground left to right. Hougoumont is just visible in the dip to the left of the tree-line on the other side.

French cavalry attack British squares from the film 'Waterloo'. [Columbia Pictures]

once; and the round-shot penetrating the column carried confusion throughout its extent. The ground already encumbered with victims of the first struggle, became almost impassable…the discharge of every gun was followed by a fall of men and horses like that of grass before the mower's scythe. When the horse alone was killed, we could see the cuirassiers divesting themselves of the encumbrance and making their escape on foot'.

Mercer's men, unlike the norm for horse artillery crews, stood their ground and held the enemy at bay by the intensity of their fire, choosing not to seek safety within the infantry squares.

The French cavalry flowed across the road at this standpoint and were then deflected between the infantry squares standing firm behind. Ensign Rees Howell Gronow of the 1st Foot Guards described the dismal conditions from within the squares:

'When we received the cavalry, the order was to fire low so that on the first discharge of musketry, the ground was strewn with the fallen horses and their riders, which impeded the advance of those behind them, and broke the shock of the charge. It was pitiful to witness the agony of the poor horses, which really seemed conscious of the danger that surrounded them. We often saw a poor wounded animal raise its head, as if looking for its rider to afford him aid….'

'During the battle our squares presented a shocking sight. Inside we were nearly suffocated by the smoke and smell from burnt cartridges. It was impossible to move a yard without treading upon a wounded comrade, or upon the bodies of the dead, dying and mutilated soldiers. The charges of cavalry were in appearance very formidable, but in reality a great relief, as the artillery could no longer fire on us'.[24]

The view from Napoleon's vantage point near La Belle Alliance of the direction of the Imperial Guard attack, just to the left of the Lion's Mound in the distance.

were targeted by artillery and cavalry. De Mauduit's unit continued to attract heavy fire:

'The balls, shells, and a little later, the case-shot, inflicted terrible losses. Nevertheless [the unit] did not abandon its post; it only re-dressed its ranks as each salvo opened a gap, firing at hardly a quarter range, and soon 150 grenadiers out of 550 were struck down'. [25]

With the repulse of the Imperial Guard, the remainder of the French Army began to disintegrate as ever larger numbers of Prussian units plunged into its right flank.

The inn at La Belle Alliance'

8 SITE OF THE FRENCH IMPERIAL GUARD ATTACK

This area is on the lane, just west of the Lion's Mound. At about 19.30 three huge columns of Napoleon's Imperial Guard marched up the same slope already churned into liquid mud by thousands of cavalry. The British Foot Guards lying in the sunken lane were suddenly ordered to stand up and opened a volley of point-blank fire that momentarily checked the lead column. They were caught in the flank off to the right by the 52nd Light Infantry and charged head on with the bayonet. The French Guard broke and fled in some disorder. Captain Harry Weyland Powell watched it all happen from the centre of the Foot Guards line:

'They continued to advance till within 50 or 60 paces of our front, when the brigade was ordered stand up. whether it was from the sudden and unexpected appearance of a corps so near them, which must have seemed as starting out of the ground, or the tremendously heavy fire we threw into them, "La Garde", who had never before failed in an attack, suddenly stopped. Those who, from a distance and more on the flank, could see the affair, tell us that the effect of our fire seemed to force the head of the column bodily back.

'In less than a minute above 300 were down. They now wavered, and several of the rear divisions began to draw out as if to deploy, whilst some of the men in their rear beginning to fire over the heads of those in front was so evident a proof of their confusion, that Lord Saltoun… holloaed out "Now's the time, my boys". Immediately the Brigade sprang forward.'

Sergeant Hippolyte de Mauduit an Imperial Guard grenadier recalled the Middle Guard battalions having been repelled, tried to reorganize:

'These valiant and unhappy survivors retired, nevertheless, still in good order, but quivering with rage, to the foot of the slope; they had lost their numerical force but not their courage'.

This left the Old Guard isolated on the left of the line and they

9 LA BELLE ALLIANCE

Position nine can be reached by either moving south-east along the track in front of the Lion's Mound or via a short drive, turning right at the traffic light cross-roads onto the Brussels road and continuing to the white Inn building on the horizon. Just to the right (north east) of the Inn is the small mound that Napoleon occupied as a vantage point during the battle. He reviewed his troops from here during the morning, the Imperial Guard marched by here at the climax of the battle and Wellington met Blücher outside the Inn at 9 pm that night.

Napoleon had been exasperated by the pessimism voiced by some of his Peninsula War marshals as they discussed their chances of victory, at breakfast just down the road at Le Caillou. He said:

'Because you have been beaten by Wellington, you consider him a great general. And now I tell you that Wellington is a bad general, that the English are bad troops, and that this affair is nothing more serious than eating one's breakfast'.

'I earnestly hope so' responded Napoleon's Chief of Staff, Marshal Soult.

That same night Wellington was to recall:

'Blucher and I met near La Belle Alliance; we were both on horseback; but he embraced and kissed me, exclaiming "Mein lieber Kamerad" and then "Quelle affaire!" which was pretty much all he knew of French'. [26]

24. Mercer, Journal of the Waterloo Campaign, P. 174-5. Gronow, C Hibbert, Waterloo, P. 216-17.
25. Powell, Brett-James, P. 160-1. De Mauduit, AW Field, Waterloo. The French Perspective, P. 206 and 208.
26. Napoleon, Hibbert, P. 193. Wellington, Ibid, P. 235.

Epic spectacle – Thousands star in Waterloo

WATERLOO (1929)

The film *Waterloo* is a 1929 black and white silent German film directed by Karl Grune. It stars Charles Vanel as Napoleon, Otto Gebühr as Marshal Blücher and Humberston Wright as Wellington. The projected pro-German stance is a response to Abel Gance's more impressive French epic *Napoleon* produced in 1927, a similar subject but on a far greater scale.

Otto Gebühr portrays a sympathetic Blücher, clearly revered by his men in the 1929 version of *Waterloo*.

Grune's film covers the victory at Waterloo through the eyes of the Allied monarchs. Charles Willy Kayser plays the Prussian Friedrich Wilhelm III, but the real hero is a warm and humane Blücher, sympathetically played by Gebühr, clearly devoted to his soldiers. Napoleon has a menacing though

Charles Vanel plays Napoleon in the 1929 version of *Waterloo*.

intermittent presence in the first half hour of the film and then virtually disappears. Wellington receives even less coverage. Despite being labelled the 'Iron Duke' he appears to be visibly under pressure until he gets the message that Blücher is finally coming. He then steels himself to hold out until rescue.

Historical authenticity is not one of the film's strong points. It does dwell on the battle at Ligny but time lapses between key events are unclear. There are some memorable images, such as rays of light coming through the forest shroud to fall like benediction on Prussian troops advancing to Wellington's rescue. Cameras pan from on high above the battlefield and transition to low level, focussing gradually on soldiers engaged in hand to hand combat. Some modern techniques are employed in this silent version but the fighting seems considerably stylised. It provides an interesting contrast to the 1970 version, but not really worth a viewing.

WATERLOO (1970)

Sergei Bondarchuk made the first authentic and arguably only significant film about the Battle of Waterloo. So vast was the £12m project that it became a co-production between the Italian Dino De Laurentiis Cinematogafica Company and the Russian Mosfilm. It was filmed on location in Rome and Caserta in Italy and Uzghorod in the Soviet Ukraine Russia. Rod Steiger plays a clearly ailing Napoleon pitted against Christopher Plummer's cool and phlegmatic Wellington.

Considerable effort was required to recreate a convincing battlefield. The Russians

20,000 Red Army extras starred in Waterloo.

bulldozed two hills, deepened a valley, laid five miles of roads, transplanted 5,000 trees and reconstructed four historic buildings. Fields of rye, barley and wild flowers were sown all around. Nearly 20,000 soldiers of the Red Army and a full brigade of Soviet militia cavalry participated in the 48 days of battle filming outside Uzghorod in stiflingly hot weather. Without the Red army the film would have cost three times as much. Two thousand additional men had to be taught to load and fire the 19th Century vintage-type muskets used at Waterloo.

Sergei Bondarchuk was a consummate logistician and an acknowledged master of the historical epic. He was a Hollywood Academy Award winner and had been awarded the Order of Lenin for his direction of the 1968 Russian version of *'War and Peace'* , which employed a staggering 120,000 extras. Bondarchuk was similarly adept in handling the huge action sequences for *Waterloo*. Soviet units led by their officers received direction from hand held radios. Battle scenes were simultaneously filmed from ground level and 100-foot scaffold towers with five panavision cameras. The crack Moscow Militia Cavalry, renowned throughout the Soviet Union, portrayed the Scot's Greys remarkable cavalry charge. Its sweeping slow motion beauty attempts to replicate the famous Lady

The charge of the Royal Scot's Greys was filmed from a railway running alongside the action, stable enough to capture the scene in panavision slow-motion. [Columbia Pictures]

Butler painting, and was filmed from panavision cameras mounted on trucks, helicopters and a railway locomotive that sped alongside the galloping riders. Other cavalry scenes employed additional Soviet horsemen and Yugoslav stuntmen.

Any problems with *Waterloo's* historical accuracy are sins of omission. The film follows the correct sequence of events and portrays all the main historical players. There is cursory treatment of the formative battles of Ligny and Quatre-Bras, but they are included. Despite its steep slopes, the battlefield valley looks authentic with all the farms in the right place. The siege of Hougoumont is handled simply as a scenic backdrop, with none of the drama of its near capture. The impact of British concentrated musketry on the Imperial Guard's final attack at the film's climax is only cursorily handled. The undefeated elite Guard appears to run away after only a few rounds. The Prussians suddenly appear at the end and give the erroneous impression that the battle was decided before their arrival; the drama of their fight for Plancenoit village is omitted. Despite the omissions, the spectacle is hauntingly effective. British and French cavalry charges are impressive 'hell for leather' affairs raising considerable dust, hardly surprising in the 90° temperatures the cast endured in the Ukraine. In reality they were slowed by the mud. Historical accuracy is, nevertheless, broadly sound relative to many commercial Hollywood interpretations of the past.

Waterloo is a film of inherent contradictions. It has a quality look with beautifully muted colours, realistic detail and artistic compositional control. Many frames are stand alone pieces in themselves. Even so, the tendency to emulate famous Waterloo paintings like Meissonier and Lady Butler and others detracts from the power of the main story line. Epic images are not necessarily supported by a terse script.

Varying acting performances mirror some of these contradictions. Wellington is superbly under-played by Christopher Plummer, playing authentically to a cool massive ego supplemented by a sharply humorous wit. An arching eyebrow or demonstrative twist of the mouth says it all. Rod Steiger's portrait of Napoleon's failing physical and mental powers is by contrast over-played. Bondarchuk's camera focusses too intently on the narrowing eyes, saggy skin, hunch back and podgy man's walk. Steiger radiates military and political fervour and dominates his scenes but the obsession with destiny is overdone. Napoleon's staff are woodenly played, although Dan O'Herlity's portrait of Marshal Ney struggling with his inner demons is effective. Ney was reputedly suffering from combat stress, having commanded Napoleon's rear-guards during the retreat from Moscow in 1812. Jack Hawkins successfully plays a hard-bitten General Picton and Orson Welles does a remarkably human job on the fat, gout-ridden Louis XVIII; bringing him sympathetically to life. By contrast Sergei Zakhariadze's caricature of Blücher, with his 'Raise the black flag, 'tzhildren' as he races to Wellington's aid to the accompaniment of 'Deutschland Über Alles' borders on the farcical. Yet the grand orchestral pieces that accompany the epic battle scenes are not dissimilar to the way Tchaikovsky orchestrates his own '1812' and is atmospherically done.

Waterloo released in 1970 has undeniable qualities, in particular the memorable aerial shots of British squares surrounded by whirlpools of French cavalry. The film was, however, a commercial flop, recovering barely $1.4m of its original $25m outlay. It has since become a must-buy and successful DVD for serious Napoleonic buffs and is well worth a view for its epic action sequences, using thousands of live extras rather than enhanced digital effects. It has aged well and no film has equalled its visual detail of the Napoleonic age, before or since.

Thousands of live extras gave Bondarchuk's film its epic painting-like quality, with wide angle shots taken from the air. [Columbia Pictures]

THE ROAD TO STALINGRAD

Hitler launched Operation *Barbarossa*, the invasion of Russia, on 22nd June 1941 and announced *'The World will hold its breath'*. After the short Blitzkrieg campaigns in Poland, France and the Balkans the aim was to settle Russia in eight to ten weeks. *'Kick in the door and the whole rotten edifice would come crumbling down'* Hitler claimed. Three German Army Groups numbering 3.6 million Germans attacked an unknown Soviet quantity believed to number between two to nine million men. Within two months of the invasion German intelligence hastily revised its estimates of Soviet strength from a projected 200 divisions upwards to 360.

By December 1941 the Wehrmacht was at the gates of Moscow having inflicted three million casualties on the Russians at a cost of half a million to itself. Success had, however, been pyrrhic, burning out 30 full division equivalents, a greater number than had invaded with Army Group North. Most importantly the cream of its leadership and veteran combat troops had fallen in this, the longest campaign of the Wehrmacht to date. All that was required was one more exhausted effort, Moscow was nearly theirs.

The Soviet counter offensive that emerged from the frozen mists of the worst Russian winter for years achieved complete strategic and operational surprise. The German front was rolled back, fighting desperate rearguards in temperatures of -35° centigrade almost to Smolensk, the half way point to Moscow, reached the previous September. There was a crisis of confidence in the German High Command. Hitler appointed himself Commander in Chief and issued the 'Hold Order'. There would be no further retreats, units were to fight and if necessary die in place. By March the front had stabilised. Hitler took personal pride in his proven ability to master a crisis, which was to have portents for the future. Most of his senior commanders were cashiered. The object was achieved but the Wehrmacht's future initiative was irretrievably compromised. Hitler no longer trusted the judgement of the German General Staff. He was convinced lost ground would be regained in the summer of 1942.

Germany had lost nearly a million men by March 1942 but had inflicted three to four times that many casualties on the enemy. She still held the fertile Ukraine, half the Soviet bread basket and cut steel and iron ore production for the beleaguered Soviet Union by three-quarters. Nazi Germany had four times more industrial capacity at its disposal than the Russians but lacked oil, being dependent upon

The Germans invaded Russia on the 21st June 1941, anticipating an eight week campaign.

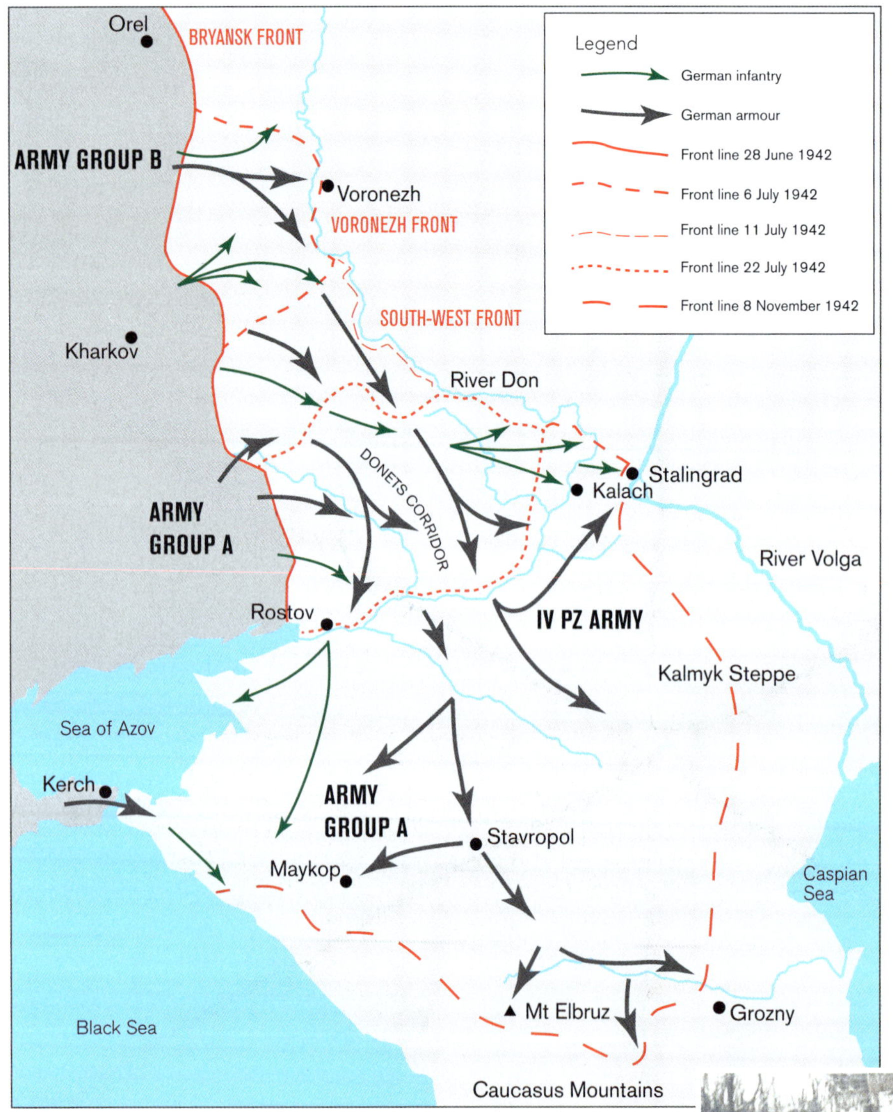

With Army Group A penetrating the Caucasus Mountains and Army Group B's Sixth Army at the gates of Stalingrad, Operation Blue launched in June 1942 represented the high tide of the Wehrmacht's eastward advance.

us that if our future operations are as successful' wrote Sixth Army German infantryman Wilhelm Hoffman in his diary *'we'll soon reach the Volga, take Stalingrad and then the war will inevitably soon be over'.*[2]

At the vanguard of *Operation Blau* was the Sixth Army commanded by the newly appointed General Friedrich von Paulus. These were the men who had stormed through Poland, France and the Ukraine the year before, and had never known defeat. The Soviets fell back in disarray across the southern Steppes, losing 600,000 men in the process. Stalin after the catastrophes of 1941 was finally convinced by his senior commanders of the logic of trading space for time. The apparent lack of resistance compared to the previous year convinced Hitler by July that *'the Russian is finished'*. Based on an unshakeable belief in the infallibility of his own judgement, proven the winter before, Hitler resolved to change Plan *Blau*. Army Group South was split into two parts to achieve its original sequential objectives at the same time. Army Group A was despatched with the bulk of the Fourth Panzer Army to immediately seize the Caucasus oilfields while Army Group B, Paulus's Sixth Army, was directed against Stalingrad on the Volga. The General Staff had thought the distances for *Blau* even before the operation began were too far and the forces too weak.

Sixth Army's advance slowed dramatically after Paulus lost fuel and panzer support. The unfortunate decision was reversed to some extent when some panzers were redirected

the Romanian Ploesti oilfields. *Operation Blau* (Blue) was launched on 28th June to destroy the Soviet armies in the south, deny Russia further resources and seize the Russian oil fields in the Caucasus. *'If I do not get the oil of Maikop and Grozny, then I must end this war'* Hitler declared.[1]

The Russian premier Joseph Stalin was convinced Hitler's next blow would be against Moscow, hundreds of miles to the north. Instead the German intention was to strike south east to encircle Soviet forces between the rivers Don and Volga. Once the Volga was cut near Stalingrad, denying the Russians its industrial and transportation centre, Army Group South would swing south into the Caucasus and seize the precious oil fields. Sixty-eight German divisions including nine panzer with 22 Allied divisions numbering 1.3 million men supported by 1,500 aircraft would advance across a 500 mile front in a very ambitious offensive. Total surprise was achieved again; Rostov-on-Don fell in less than a month as Soviet opposition appeared to disintegrate. *'The company commander told*

By the Russian winter in 1941-2 the German Army had lost a million men, which included the cream of its junior leadership and combat troops.

Below right: By late August German tanks stood on the banks of the Volga north of Stalingrad

Below left: Operation Blau launched in June 1942 seemed to roll effortlessly across the Russian Steppes. Close Luftwaffe air support for the panzers was key.

north to support him, but offensive momentum had stalled. Retreating Soviet forces managed to avoid encirclement outside Stalingrad and escaped into the city. Time lost in August had been used to bolster its defences. On the 9th August the panzers reached the oil fields at Maikop, only to find them ruined and on fire.

Two weeks later German mountain soldiers scaled the 18,500 foot summit of Mount Elbruz in the Caucasus. This was the pinnacle of success for Hitler's expansion into Europe. The III Reich now stretched from Brittany in the west to the Caucasus Mountains in the east, from the North Cape of Norway to North Africa in the south. On the 23rd August the Sixth Army reached the outskirts of Stalingrad, its 16th Panzer Division penetrated to the banks of the Volga north of the city. They were at the gateway to Asia.

Stalingrad was one of the most vibrant cities in southern Russia, the show-piece of the Soviet Union. Its citizens strolled through leafy boulevards and parks alongside the Volga River in the city that bore its premier's name. Huge factories were

still producing material for the Russian war effort. As the German divisions closed in the Luftwaffe started its colossal air onslaught: 2,000 aircraft sorties dropped 1,000 tons of bombs in 48 hours, more than at the height of the London Blitz. Neighbourhoods of wooden worker's houses were transformed into blazing infernos, in which 25,000 Russian civilians perished. A pall of ominous smoke from burning oil rose three and a half kilometres into the sky over the city. Approaching German soldiers thought it resembled a sinister black cross. The battle for Stalingrad was about to begin.

1. Hitler, W.Goerlitz , *Paulus and Stalingrad*, 1963, P. 155.
2. Hoffman, V Chuikov, *The Beginning of the Road*, 1963, P. 248.

THE END OF WEHRMACHT INVINCIBILITY

THE BATTLE FOR STALINGRAD 1941/42

The city of Stalingrad was 30 to 40 miles long and about five miles wide backing onto the broad Volga river, which was over a mile and a half wide in places. With its dense northern factory area, civic and park centre including the dominating Mamayev Kurgan hill mass and residential area to the south, Stalingrad was too large to encircle. General von Paulus therefore resolved upon four to five frontal attacks to divide the city into segments, which would then be eliminated piece-meal. He was poised to assault with 200,000 men, 500 panzers and 4,000 guns. Sixth Army had four infantry and two panzer corps at its disposal: 20 German and two Romanian divisions. Opposing him was about 54,000 Soviet troops from 62nd Army which formed part of the Stalingrad Front commanded by Colonel General Yeremenko. On 12th September General Vasily Chuikov was appointed commander of 62nd Army. He had about 100 tanks in the city and 1,000 artillery pieces, mainly ranged along the opposite bank of the Volga River.

Even as the opposing forces gathered General Georgi Zhukov, Stalin's recently appointed deputy, was developing a counter offensive plan. Arriving in the city on 29th August he saw that further counter attacks with the available resources would be futile. Stalingrad had to be held but in the context of a wider strategic plan. Time was needed while the STAVKA, (the Supreme Soviet command) amassed sufficient reserves for a future counter offensive. Operation *Uranus* was evolved to surround the German salient even now approaching the city. An even wider scheme: Operation *Saturn* was developed to destroy the exposed Army Group A in the Caucasus. These breathtakingly ambitious decisions were taken at the very lowest point of Soviet fortunes.

Two weeks after devastating Luftwaffe air raids reduced the city to impassable areas of entangled rubble, Paulus launched an all out assault on 14th September. Von-Seydlitz-Kurbach's 51st Corps tore into the northern and central sectors of the city in two pincers, designed to reach the Volga and turn inwards along the bank to surround the defenders. Below the Tsaritsa River in southern Stalingrad similar pincer attacks were launched. The primary focus was to capture the ferry landing jetties in the centre of the city to prevent Russian reinforcement and take the dominating heights of the Mamayev Kurgan. It was assumed the city would quickly fall, but six German battalion commanders and many company commanders were killed on the first day alone as company strengths were quickly whittled down to 50%. Reeling under the initial onslaught and despite inflicting serious casualties it looked as though the Russians might be swept away.

Chuikov, the Russian commander sent General Rodimtsev's 10,000 strong 13th Guards Division across the Volga River on 15th September in an attempt to restore a critical situation. The central railway station changed hands four times that day and 15 times by 19th September.

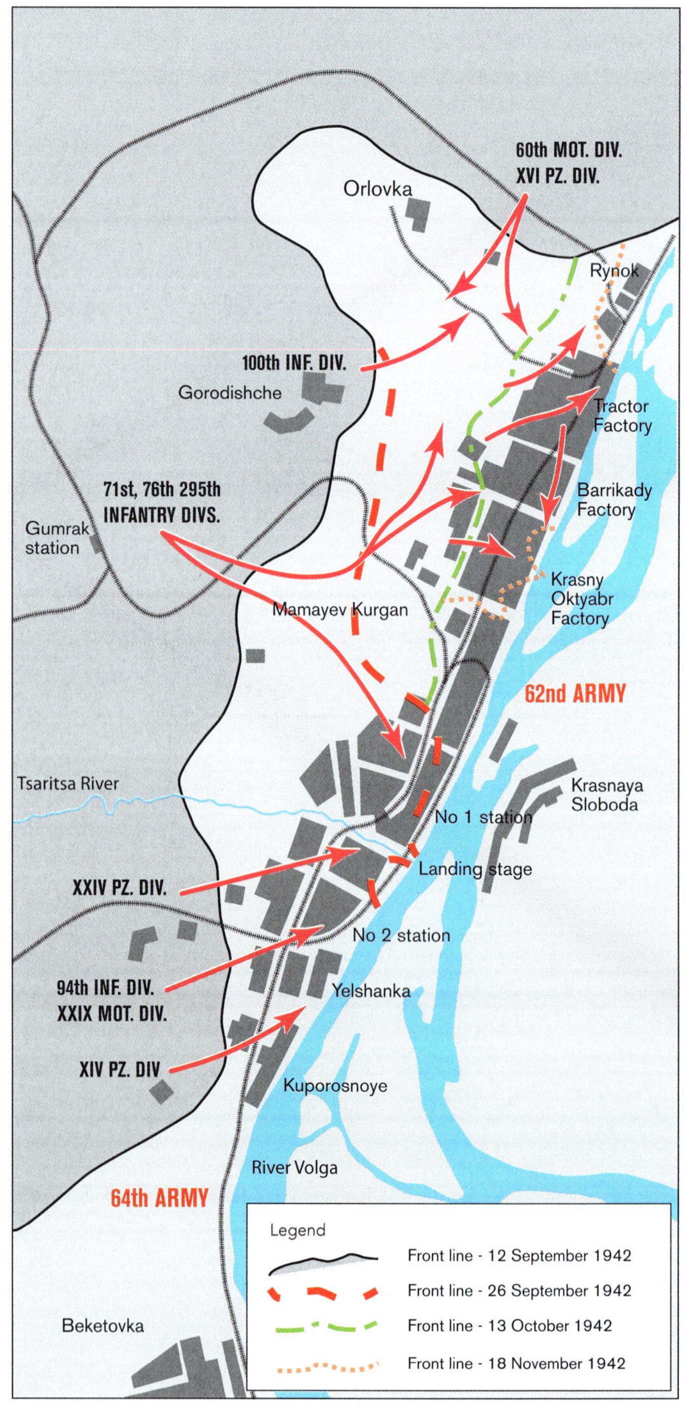

General von Paulus opted for frontal attacks along the length of Stalingrad to divide the city into segments that could be eliminated piece-meal.

A last drag on a cigarette before the advance into the ruined factory district.

Within a week 80% of the division was dead or wounded but the line was temporarily held. *'We received a 25-man reinforcement, only five or six were left after four days'* Sixth Army Infantryman Vincenz Griesemer recalled, *'they didn't listen to our advice and keep their heads down'* he ruefully commented. *'Make a mistake and you didn't need any rations'.*[3] By the 26th September central and southern Stalingrad was in German hands.

Chuikov commanding the defence intuitively appreciated that the broken terrain of Stalingrad's urban ruins would impede the combined arms effectiveness of German infantry, panzers and Luftwaffe, that had proved so clinically effective on the open steppes. *'Grab them by the belt'* Chuikov ordered and engaged the enemy so closely that the Luftwaffe could not support, for fear of hitting their own troops. German panzers could not manoeuvre and became vulnerable to infantry anti-tank weapons. He urged:

'Get close to the enemy's positions. Move on all fours, making use of craters and ruins. Carry your tommy-gun on your shoulder. Take ten to twelve grenades. Timing and surprise will be on your side…into the

'Rake it with your Tommy-gun! And get a move on!'

building – a grenade! A turning – another grenade! Rake it with your Tommy-gun! And get a move on!'[4]

On 27th September the German focus of attacks switched to the northern factory area. Eleven infantry divisions supported by 150 panzers reached the outer fringes of the Red October tractor factory. They were fought to a standstill amid a wasteland of twisted metal frames and collapsed factory walls. Surrounded Soviet strong-points fought to the last, refusing to submit and broke up German attacks by directing massed artillery fire from Russian guns lining the east bank of the Volga. They were positioned at a density of 160 per mile, supported by 200 heavy long range Katyusha lorry mounted multiple rocket systems.

Von Paulus launched an all-out assault on 27th September 1942 on the Factory District of Stalingrad. An air and artillery bombardment, shown here, preceded the attack.

The Luftwaffe mounted its largest effort yet on 5th October with 2,000 sorties against the northern factory complex. Follow-up infantry attacks stalled among the workshops of the tractor factory with the Soviets holding on to the worker's bath houses. Another push was mounted on the 14th October when three infantry divisions supported by 300 panzers and specialist Engineer assault battalions attacked with almost 90,000 men over a three mile front. They penetrated about a mile reaching the Volga at isolated points. Russian enclaves shrunk to three or four, perched on the steep banks of the Volga itself. Attacks petered out ten days later and were briefly resurrected on 9th November when five veteran German Assault Pioneer battalions tried to eradicate the final strong-points with flamethrowers and satchel charges. Within 24 hours only one man in five was still on his feet. Paulus had destroyed about 75% of Chuikov's 62nd Army, but the remnants were still clinging to the west bank of the Volga.

Hitler had announced to the world at a Munich party rally the previous day that Stalingrad had, to all intents, fallen. *'I wanted to take it and, you know, we are being modest, for we have got it!'* Only a few strong points remained. Shivering lice-ridden German troops huddling over their radios in the ruins of Stalingrad shook their heads in disbelief. Temperatures were falling. The first ice was forming on the Volga, impeding the passage of Soviet ferries.

Regrouping in the factory district of the ruined city.

Despair is etched on the faces of these soldiers seeking rescue from the encircled pocket by the Luftwaffe, who could only fly in less than half their daily requirement.

German Army intelligence had identified a build up of Soviet forces opposite Third Romanian Army, securing the Stalingrad salient flanks since the end of October. By early November the reports became disturbing. Then, on the 19th November the Soviet storm, Operation *Uranus*, finally broke. Six Soviet armies from the South West and Don Fronts collapsed the Romanian line across a 200 mile front to the north of the Stalingrad salient. Twenty-four hours later another three armies from Yeremenko's Stalingrad Front overwhelmed the Romanian forces on the southern flank. The northern and southern Russian pincers met at Kalach on the Don River on 23rd November, completely encircling the German Sixth Army within a *Kessel* or 'cauldron' pocket. Seven Soviet armies numbering 97 divisions enclosed the Germans within an area measuring 80 miles long by 25 to 35 miles wide.

To surround such a large unit without warning was incomprehensible to the Germans. Only 100 panzers had been serviceable in the sub-arctic conditions when the counter-offensive broke. Hitler ordered the troops inside the pocket to fight in place in the over optimistic belief that air re-supply would suffice, until a break-out attempt could be mounted by Field Marshal Manstein's newly formed Army Group Don. Food, fuel and ammunition quickly reduced to starvation levels as the 300 tons per day promised by the Luftwaffe could at best only manage 120 tons, less than half the minimum. Winter storms and Soviet air defences crippled the airlift. In the pocket *'the hunger was so great'* recalled soldier Walter Baschnegger, *'that men were no longer completely human and comrades no longer friends'.*[5]

When on 20th December yet another Soviet offensive, a reduced version of the Operation *Saturn* planned in September, threatened the very existence of Army Group A in the Caucasus, Manstein had to abandon his under-resourced relief attempt. His vanguards had got to within 30 miles of the city and tell-tale flashes of light on the skyline were poignantly viewed by the emaciated troops in Stalingrad during the run up to Christmas. Stalingrad was sacrificed to save Army Group A, which began to retreat along an increasingly threatened corridor at the end of December.

The last Soviet attacks on the pocket began on 10th January 1943, soon overrunning the final surviving German airfields. General Paulus, a broken man, moved his headquarters from an outlying village into the Univermag department store in central Stalingrad. Hitler promoted him to Field Marshal on 31st January, hoping he would opt for a hero's suicide, but he surrendered the same day. Within 48 hours his starving soldiers had ceased fighting. Hitler was politically humiliated. The total defeat of his biggest and most successful army signalled that the Wehrmacht aura of apparent invincibility was broken.

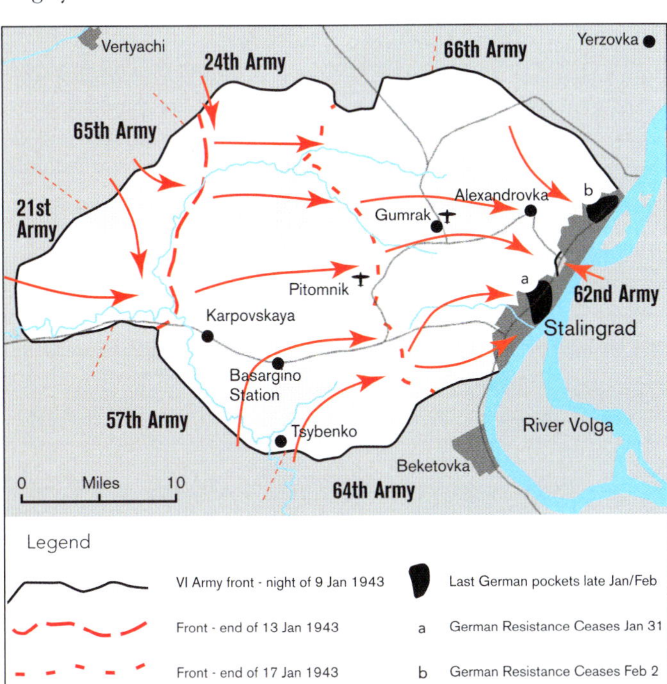

The relief of Stallingrad: the final Russian push to liberate Stallingrad lasted three weeks

Starving German soldiers are marched off into captivity. Only 5,000 of over the 100,000 captured were going to return home.

3. Griesmer, G Knopp, *Stalingrad. Das Drama*, P. 142.
4. Chuikov, Alan Clark article, Purnell's History of the Second World War, Vol 3, P. 1146.
5. Baschnegger, Knopp, P. 244.

Hesitancy versus...

FIELD MARSHAL VON PAULUS: COMMANDER SIXTH ARMY

The newly appointed commander of the German Sixth Army, General Friedrich von Paulus was a competent staff officer, but not an inspiring leader of men. He was completely loyal to Adolf Hitler, whose teachings and political success he admired. Hitler after initially nurturing his career was to eventually dismiss him as too intellectual with insufficient character.

Von Paulus (centre with goggles) directs operations against Stalingrad, and on surrendering (below) on 30th January 1943. He transitioned from near victory to catastrophe in three months.

Paulus was 52 years old at the battle of Stalingrad. Born into a middle class family he married into the Romanian aristocracy. He was a staff officer at heart and served as such during the First World War. Assessment reports during his early *Reichswehr* career in the 1920s speak of a highly competent desk officer who *'lacked decisiveness'* during practical troop manoeuvres. An enigmatic figure, he projected an elegant and cool staff façade with an impressive eye for meticulous staff detail. His students at *Infanterieschule V* during an infantry school teaching appointment nick-named him *'the ditherer.'* [6]

By September 1939 he was the Tenth Army Chief of Staff (COS) during the Polish campaign and later COS to General von Reichenau during the French *Blitzkrieg* in 1940. He was the perfect intellectual foil to the brash, energetic and decisive Reichenau. Paulus came to Hitler's attention during the planning for Operation Barbarossa in 1941, when he was Halder's Deputy Chief of Staff. He was renowned for his ability to minutely study every situation before issuing orders down to the smallest detail. He was essentially rewarded for his staff expertise when he was appointed Commander Sixth Army in January 1942, taking over from his feisty former superior von Reichenau.

Without realising it, Paulus had been promoted way beyond his practical experience and capabilities. As one of the youngest of the army commanders he had never commanded a division or corps, or any combat unit in action. Yet he effectively mastered his first crisis, defeating Marshal Timoshenko's unexpected Kharkov spring offensive just prior to the launch of Operation *Blau*. A good start, for which he was rewarded with the Knight's Cross. His subsequent advance to Stalingrad was dogged by fuel shortages because of Hitler's unexpected change of plan. By late September he was engaged in a battle of attrition for the city that bore Stalin's name, and had Hitler's undivided attention.

With limited practical experience von Paulus had few creative solutions for the impasse, other than applying even more force with every set back. His logic was to frontally attack the long thin city and carve it up into digestible enclaves. The plan was frustrated at every turn by stubbornly held strong-points, which fought on despite being surrounded, and by Chuikov's creative and aggressive low-level tactics.

Paulus exercised command from well back, in a village 30 miles to the west of Stalingrad. The fastidious general detested dirt and washed and changed his clothes daily, while his louse-ridden infantry fought a *Rattenkrieg* (rat war), for possession of every ruin, sewer and hole alongside the Volga. Constant progress reports demanded by the Führer alongside incomprehensibly bitter Soviet resistance produced a nervous tic-reaction in Paulus's cheek. This is visible in the later newsreels that covered the unfolding drama.

When the command crisis erupted with a threat of Soviet encirclement after the counter-offensive on November 19th, Paulus prevaricated. By the 21st November he decided to stand after initially opting to break out. By the time Hitler ordered him to hold in place the next day his initial freedom of action had been lost dithering. By the 23rd November he was surrounded and any chance of creatively misunderstanding Hitler's intentions and breaking out regardless was lost. Hitler promised a rescue and that meanwhile he would be supplied by a Luftwaffe air-bridge. Paulus, overwhelmed by events believed him. It was not in his character to do otherwise.

Field Marshal von Manstein's rescue attempt with two under-strength corps to get him out between 12th and 19th December opened up a second window of opportunity. On this occasion the clearly reluctant and nervous Paulus deferred offensive action to link up, claiming he had insufficient fuel to bridge the 30 mile gap and that he was bound by inflexible orders from Hitler not to leave the Volga. With nothing ventured, little could be gained. There is controversy about how much lassitude he had to act. This became irrelevant in any case once further Soviet offensive activity imperilled the very existence of Army Group A. Paulus obeyed Hitler's order not to capitulate to a Soviet surrender offer on 8th January. The Stalingrad pocket was pinning down 90 major Soviet units, which would otherwise wreak havoc with the Army Group South withdrawal. Sixth Army was left to its fate.

Hitler promoted Paulus to Field Marshal on 31st January. He surrendered his staff the same day at the Univermag departmental store in the centre of Stalingrad. Paulus realised the promotion *'was truly a request to commit suicide, but I will not accede to his* [Hitler's] *wish'*. Resistance ceased two days later. [7]

Paulus did not initially cooperate with the Soviets until he heard about the execution of his friends, Generals Erich Hoepner and Erwin von Witzleben, after the abortive assassination attempt on Hitler in

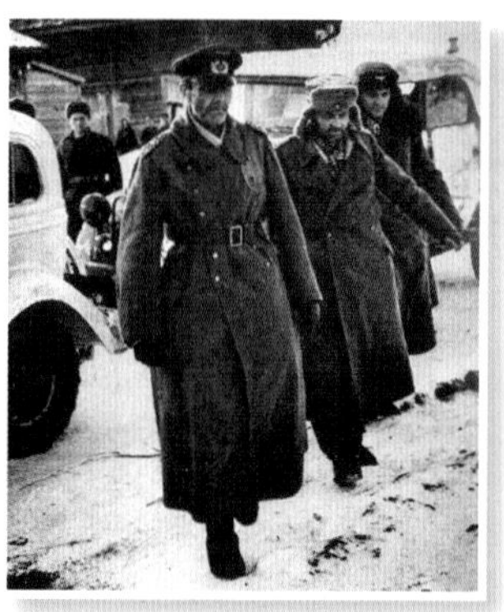

July 1944. He joined the League of German Officers in Captivity, participating in radio surrender appeals, for which Hitler imprisoned his family. Paulus appeared as a witness for the Soviet prosecution during the Nuremeberg War Trials in 1946, but was not released until 1953. His wife died at Baden-Baden four years before his return. He worked for the East German Police in the Soviet controlled part of Germany until his death on 1st February 1957.

...Aggressive resolve

General Vasily I Chuikov.

 GENERAL VASILY I CHUIKOV: COMMANDER 62ND ARMY

General Vasily Chuikov was 42 years old when he took over command of the Soviet 62nd Army on 12th September, replacing its former broken commander Lapotin, sacked 48 hours before Paulus's first all-out assault on Stalingrad. He had no illusions about what lay ahead. *'You have to save Stalingrad. How do you feel about it?'* his Front Commander Yeremenko asked him on appointment. 'It means to die. So we will die' he responded.[8]

Chuikov was the antithesis of the fastidious and aloof Paulus, the son of a peasant, he was irredeemably scruffy. He had a pugnacious fighter's face, with a broad nose and beetle brow. His father had been a wrestler. British war correspondent Alexander Werth recalled his typical bonhomie and loud laugh, which revealed *'teeth crowned in gold and they glittered in the light of the electric lights'*. Unlike Paulus he imbued 62nd Army with his own stern and indomitable will. Resistance appeared to stiffen on his very appearance. He ordered an interactive defence of mini-urban redoubts built with all-round defence linked by prowling fast moving and aggressive storm-groups. He insisted *'every German soldier must be made to feel he lives under the muzzle of a Russian gun'*.[9]

The new general's background was practical with a mixture of some staff. He joined the Red Army in 1919, fought in the Civil War and quickly rose through the ranks by virtue of his Communist Party membership. After attending the Frunze Military Academy he took part in the Russian occupation of eastern Poland in 1939 and the Russo-Finish war the following year. He was unsullied by the early Russian failures following the German invasion because he was acting as military advisor to China's Chiang Kai-Shek. In May 1942 he was recalled.

Paulus was never able to effectively impose his will on this battle, Chuikov did from the start. He could be ruthless and unforgiving with subordinates that failed him. Soviet war reporter Vasily Grossman saw him punch subordinates in a foul mood commenting he was *'as ready to execute a brigade commander who failed in his duty as a simple soldier who turned tail in battle, but his own physical bravery was beyond question'*. When his own headquarters was engulfed in blazing oil from a ruptured oil storage reservoir, Chuikov continued to direct the battle. His lined and scarred face made him look older than his 42 years and eczema developed with the stress, often requiring his hands to be bandaged, but he never faltered in his almost unrealistic belief in eventual victory.

Chuikov's biggest contribution was to adapt the street fighting techniques his men employed to cope with the urban moonscape for which they had to fight. The Germans were perplexed at their inability to tactically manoeuvre with their traditional technical superiority and bogged themselves down in a battle of attrition. Chuikov formed mobile storm groups able to quickly attack with grenades, sub-machine guns, sharpened spades and flamethrowers. They operated between killing zones established by strong-points, which fought to the death above and below ground.

Chuikov (second from left) directing his staff from the command bunker in Stalingrad. His chief commissar Gurov is sitting to his right.

Chuikov held the city while Stalin's deputy Zhukov assembled reserves for the unexpected counter offensive that was launched on November 19th. He bitterly resented Zhukov not confiding in him about Operation *Uranus* until virtually the last moment. It gave the impression that far from being the prime architect of the destruction of the German Sixth Army, 62nd Army was in effect a tethered goat enabling General Rokossovsky's Don Front to deliver a mobile *coup de grace*.

After Stalingrad, Chuikov was to follow an illustrious career. He was promoted to command 8th Guards army, which he was to lead to Berlin by 1945. In 1955 he was made a Marshal of the Soviet Union and appointed Chief of Soviet Ground Forces between 1960-4. He died ten years after retirement in 1982 and was the first Soviet Marshal to be interred outside Moscow, fittingly within the Mamayev Kurgan memorial complex overlooking the city he saved at Volgograd.

6. Reports and nickname, FW von Mellenthin, *Deutschlands Generale des Zweiten Weltkriegs*, 1977, P. 104-5.
7. Paulus, G Knopp, *Hitlers Krieger*, P. 279.
8. Chuikov, Ed A Beevor & L Vinogradova, *A Writer at War. V Grossman*. P.144.
9. Chuikov, *The Beginning of the Road*, 1963, P. 80.

'when you have to look into the eyes of dead comrade'

THE SIXTH ARMY GERMAN SOLDIER

There was little hurrah patriotism in the ranks of the German Sixth Army and no artificial Nazi propaganda and feelings concerning the likely outcome of this war were mixed. The average *Landser* (German equivalent to 'Tommy') was inclined to be cynical. He was well trained, hardy and frugal, aggressive in attack and steadfast in defence. The Sixth Army had only experienced victory thus far in Poland, France and the Ukraine. Set backs had occurred but not defeat. As the motorised formations poured across the sun-baked Russian steppe, once again the Volga River, the gateway to Asia, came into sight. They had defeated a Soviet spring offensive weeks before. Even the most pessimistic could consider a possible end to this war having reached the Volga. But as they penetrated the city of Stalingrad along its banks, Russian resistance stiffened.

The German army had changed in character since the start of the Russian campaign. Most men were indifferent to propaganda but many were becoming increasingly disillusioned with their inability to fight the Russian to submission. Unlike the western armies, the Russians fought to the death and did not surrender when encircled. The cream of the German officers and NCOs in the combat arms had died in the course of the previous year and more than a third had perished. Training times of six to 18 months meant they were virtually irreplaceable. Virtually all the World War I veterans, the youngest being in their early forties, were dead or worn out. Their replacements were younger, less compromising men, who had been educated under National Socialism or owed recent advancement to it. New officers and NCOs continued to lead from the front, but were less schooled in auftragstaktik, the creative mix of mission orientated tactics that encouraged initiative. The new men were less adept at thinking their way out of tough situations.[10]

The will to fight was being eroded by fearsome casualties and increasing reports of heavy allied bombing of their loved ones, hundreds of miles away at home. The average Landser did his duty. He saw the atrocities, to their shame, being inflicted by the SS in rear areas but was still convinced he belonged to the best army in the world. They were now to be engulfed in the largest and most intense urban battle they had ever experienced.

These gaunt-looking German infantry nearing Stalingrad had campaigned hard and marched hundreds of miles across the sun-baked southern steppe before even reaching Stalingrad. Physical reserves were low and intestinal problems rife.

The strain of weeks of highly intense and costly street fighting is etched on the faces of these young men who are resigned to a likely limited future.

The typical soldier respected and feared the Russian. Some of the younger and more ideologically orientated hated him. *'I wouldn't wish my worst enemy to fight against the Russian'*, admitted Georg Buchwald, *'he was the worst soldier I ever fought against'*. German soldiers were dismayed at the profligate waste of life by Russian human wave assaults, conducted by *'savage drunk'* Russian soldiers. The worse fear was to be captured. *'We saw badly mutilated corpses of some of our men who had been overrun when they lay wounded in a dressing station'* Buchwald recalled. Not so unusual, war on the Eastern Front was truly total. At Stalingrad it surpassed all norms. Company commander Joachim Stempel with Panzer Grenadier Regiment 103 lost 17 men killed and 33 wounded from his one hundred strong company in three days. Replacements lasted barely 24 hours.

Stempel described seven days fighting through the northern factory area between 25th October and 1st November. At one stage he was the only officer left in his regiment, apart from the battalion commander. Multiple Russian counter-attacks occurred each day. White flares were fired to identify indistinct urban front lines to supporting Stuka dive bombers. Red flares went up in desperation if they had to bring down their own artillery fire onto their positions if Russian attacks threatened to overwhelm them. It was only possible to defecate in the helmets of dead men and throw them outside the holes they fought and lived in all day. Casualties occurred the moment they broke cover. Movement and the recovery of the wounded could only take place after dusk; even then food carriers were constantly ambushed and killed by Soviet stay-behind groups, as they tried to make their way forward. Vincenz Griesmer recalled the nightmare of being pinned down all day *'when you have to look into the eyes of a dead comrade being used all day as a bullet-catch'*. Snipers dominated no-mans land and few prisoners were taken.[11]

The Germans had to adapt to a tactical situation completely beyond their experience. The traditional combined-arms battle with Luftwaffe and panzer support did not work effectively in man-on-man close quarter street fighting. Formal orders transitioned to hurried discussions around an air photograph huddled in cellars. Conventional infantry sections had to be reconfigured into urban assault groups, about which little was known. Soldiers became bewildered by the strange conditions in which they now fought. Leutnant Gottfried von Bismarck described fighting in a multi-storey block where the Germans held the ground floor, the Russians the first and Germans fought Russians between the third and fourth floors of the same building.

Soldiers jettisoned 60 to 80lb marching equipments to fight in skeleton harness order; it was only possible to squeeze through narrow openings carrying iron rations, ammunition and water. They fought from street to street, house to house and room to room with rifle and bayonet, Schmeisser machine-pistol, grenade and pistol as artillery pulverised streets and housing blocks all around. Some did not wash for weeks, shrouded in cloying brick dust, lice-ridden and denied hot food for days. Tinned sausage with maybe some bread and jam might come up with the ammunition re-supply. Tainted water was often the only option for men constantly pinned down by fire. By the third month of this, the body resistance and digestive systems of those

'I wouldn't wish my worst enemy to fight against the Russians'

surviving was impaired with dysentery and diarrhoea rife.

With the onset of cold weather and sub-zero temperatures with the Russian encirclement, re-supply to the front line was tenuous at best. By 9th January the daily ration allowance could fit in a trouser pocket. There was 75 grams of bread, 24 grams of vegetables and maybe 200 grams of horse flesh, with 12 grams of fat and sugar and maybe a cigarette and 9 grams of fluids – if it got through. Soldiers were actually starving to death before the surrender.

The German soldiers could not believe that an army as large as 23 divisions could be surrounded by the Russians. Neither did the Russians. They thought they had netted about 90,000 rather than the actual 250,000 men that emerged from the pocket; lack of sufficient food accounted for many of the early deaths. German soldiers believed their Führer would get them out as he promised. He did not; and with that the Wehrmacht lost its aura of invincibility. Only 91,000 survived to surrender and half of these had perished by the spring. Only 5,000 eventually came back from Soviet captivity in the early 1950s.

SNIPER MYTHS AT STALINGRAD

'Do you want to see how good the Russians can shoot?' one of Leutnant Gottfried von Bismarck's Sixth Army soldiers asked him. He stuck out a newspaper beyond the door of the factory foreman's office, where they were sitting drinking schnapps. *'There was a bang and already a hole inside the paper'*. Snipers dominated the ruined urban landscape at Stalingrad.[12]

Russian sniper Sergeant Vassily 'Vasha' Zaitsev arrived with the 284th Rifle Division at Stalingrad in September 1942. Within ten days he had despatched 40 Germans. Snipers and their exploits were talked about and admired like football stars. Propaganda accounts extolled Zaitsev as the best with 225 kills. Other snipers were to achieve scores of 400 to 500 by the end of the war. Female sniper Ludmilla Pavlichenko was credited with 309 kills. Gefreiter Matthäus Hetzenauer a German Gebirgsjäger (mountain soldier) corporal was awarded the Knight's Cross in 1945 for 345 confirmed kills.

A soviet sniper selects his next victim.

They won the 'Rattenkrieg'

Impossible conditions were endured for 'Mother Russia' and the certain knowledge that their conduct at the front had implications for their families back home. A forward observation post.

THE 62ND ARMY RUSSIAN SOLDIER

The typical Russian soldier arriving in a relief battalion for the beleaguered 62nd Army was transported near to the east bank of the Volga by train and then marched up. Afterwards he boarded one of the Volga ferries for the perilous mile crossing under German artillery and Luftwaffe air attacks. Stalingrad, covered by a sinister pall of black-oily smoke hovering over its smouldering ruins, was an intimidating prospect. The temperature rose in the glare of fires as boats neared the blazing city. War correspondent Konstantin Simonov recalled the air had *'the sad smell of burnt iron'*. The Russian soldier was psychologically stressed running the gauntlet of bomb and shell even before he stepped off the ferries onto the landing jetty. NKVD security troops manning the reception areas ensured the reinforcements only went one way, forward, into the maw of the burning city. Summary executions encouraged any that wavered. Men without rifles had to pick one up from the dead or wounded lying on the battlefield.

Russian soldiers were motivated by their desire to liberate the Motherland, an emotion that the Communist Party had re-packaged when Soviet propaganda had not sufficed. Life they were informed would get radically better after victory and soldiers and civilians alike genuinely wanted to believe in the good will of their government as well as avenge German atrocities. Many were to be disillusioned after the war. Tank officer Lieutenant Vladimir Alexeev remembered what was required: *'I must do as I am told'* he recalled. Soldiers swiftly bonded for survival in the trying conditions of Stalingrad. *'We were all one family'* Alexeev insisted, *'we treated everyone as our brother, we shared everything, never argued'*. The impact of a heart-felt allegiance to 'Mother Russia,' an unfamiliar notion to modern materially minded westerners, should not be underestimated. Sergeant Yakov Pavlov defended a strong-point house blocking German access to the Volga in central Stalingrad for 58 days; on being asked why he fought so tenaciously he responded *'Rodina* – Motherland!'[13]

Although the average soldier appeared outwardly sombre, serious and dull to foreign correspondents, scratching the surface revealed men of passion, humour and humanity. Fighting in Stalingrad was approached with a degree of equanimity, *'a person only lives once'* Alexeev explained. Russian soldiers did not have a methodical approach for what they did, they dealt with events as they occurred. They could bitterly resist and then suddenly give up. Rations were primitive, sausages and bread sometimes coming forward with the ammunition. Winter clothing was far superior to the Germans, an important factor by November.

The Commissar system stiffened resolve because every soldier was aware that any lapse in patriotism would have consequences not only at the front, but also for his family back home. Most soldiers adopted a philosophical 'live and let die' attitude toward an authoritarian system they did not consider menacing until things went wrong. If a tank was abandoned without it burning, the crew could be shot. Any man taken prisoner was considered a traitor. Discipline was fierce and this matched with an ingrained stoicism and desire not to stand out in a crowd stifled initiative, but could make the Russian soldier a stubborn and at times savage adversary. They regarded German soldiers as disciplined, men who carried out orders to the letter and were individually dogged and brave. Alexeev regarded *'the Germans at Stalingrad as very good as also the Hungarians'*, while *'the Romanians and Italians were not so good. They were all deceived by their own propaganda'*.

Soviet officers were stubbornly persistent in carrying through combat missions and displayed courage and daring. Some like Rodintsev commanding the 13th Guards Division, had been a veteran of street fighting around Madrid University during the Spanish Civil War. One weakness was a low standard of tactical training and a persistent inability to coordinate effectively with supporting and other arms units. Although they lacked the initiative and imagination for creative manoeuvre, one-on-one street fighting played to their strengths, which were tenacity and a preparedness to accept crippling casualties to achieve the mission. Lieutenant Anatoly Kozlov, an infantry officer at Stalingrad recalled his platoon had *'about 30 soldiers, very young and poorly trained, most did not know how to use a machine gun or had*

William Craig, the author of *Enemy at the Gates*, later a Hollywood film, tells the story of Zaitsev's duel with a legendary German sniper, sent to Stalingrad to eliminate him. Zaitsev alerted by Soviet sniper deaths dramatically tracks his quarry to beneath a sheet of metal in a ruined factory. He kills him after detecting the tell-tale glint of the German's telescopic sight. His adversary, Major Erwin König, later identified as Heinz Thorvald by Zaitsev himself, was the alleged chief of an equally unidentifiable SS German sniper school. None of this information is traceable in German war-time records. Despite the fact that Russian company and regimental records were faithfully kept throughout even the worse days of the Stalingrad siege, there is no duel recorded in any war diaries. This is an odd omission when the Soviet press was extolling the cult of 'sniperism'. Zaitsev never confirmed or denied the event himself. Both German names were very common at this time. They appear in Soviet war records but not on the German side. Cynics might suggest German officials erased the event because of its morale significance after a catastrophic defeat

Information shortfalls, however, in no way detract from Zaitsev's skills and those of many other Russian snipers. Their impact in dominating no-man's land contributed to rather than decisively influenced the outcome of the battle. It appears Russian sniper groups might well have possessed the edge. Russian snipers formed a standard part of infantry units and others, including the female groups, were organized into brigades, from which entire platoons, companies or even battalions might be despatched to selected fronts. Zaitsev developed tactics at Stalingrad that were adopted elsewhere, namely three teams of two men, a spotter and firer, earmarked to dominate a particular area or feature. The Russian Moisin PU telescope fitted to the Nagent 1891/30 rifle was superior to the German ZF-39 fitted to the Mauser rifle. It was weather resistant and its 3.5 magnification was superior to the German 1.5.

German snipers came from a battalion sniper group of about 22 men, with two distributed to each rifle-company and others grouped where required. Both sides hunted the observers spotting for artillery and other heavy calibre weapons, opposing commanders and important men such as machine gunners. There were complaints from the 24th Panzer Division in Stalingrad that there were insufficient sniper scopes. Russian snipers generally reigned supreme.

Snipers were not the super-human combatants that Hollywood and contemporary press accounts would have us believe. Good shots can always be found in armies numbering millions. Given a rifle with a telescopic sight and some training he becomes a better shot. Effective snipers were adept at personal camouflage and concealment and especially at judging wind and distance. The best were either philosophical or cold-blooded individuals with a lot of patience and demonstrably cool in battle.[15]

A sniper scope view peering into no-mans land near the factory district.

very little experience'. Despite losses that were five-fold higher than the Germans, *'we managed to wear them down'.*[14] Soviet assault groups fought with the PPSH 7.62 mm sub-machine gun, Tokarev pistols, stick grenades and sharpened spades. Despite often mastering the enemy in close combat, they could not match German firepower or its precise coordination and execution, for which a terrible price was paid. One in three of the 13th Guards Division died within 24 hours of crossing the Volga and only 329 were left from 10,000 in a week.

Russian artillery massed on the east bank of the Volga did much to blunt the German attacks. Chuikov's hyperactive defence conducted amid multi-storey building blocks, from which the defenders had to be levered out floor by floor, bogged down the more manoeuvrable and heavily armed German units in a battle of attrition. *'The street is no longer measured by metres but by corpses'* wrote 24th panzer officer Leutnant Wiener in his diary.

The 62nd Army defenders managed to hold onto a few enclaves on the west bank of the Volga until the Soviet counter-offensive suddenly emerged into the exhausted German rear and flanks. In psychological terms, however, the German Sixth Army had already met its match on the banks of the Volga before they were encircled. They lost the *Rattenkrieg* – 'rat war'. It was the German turn to be tactically outmanoeuvred by an opponent who had taken 18 months to learn the painful lessons of the opening campaigns.

10. R J Kershaw, *War Without Garlands*, P.176.
11. Stempel Diary, J Turner, *Stalingrad Day By Day*, P. 108-18. Griesmer, G Knopp, *Stalingrad. Das Drama*, P. 164.
12. Bismarck, G Knopp, *Stalingrad. Das Drama* , P. 142.
13. Simonov and Pavlov, B Moynahan, Forgotten Soldiers, Pp. 62 and 68. Alexeev, author interview 29 Jul 06.
14. Kozlov, author interview, 30 Jul 06.
15. Details from M Haskew, *The Sniper at War*, Pp. 65-77 and A Writer at War. V Grossman, P. 155-9.

The Bloody Fight for Stalin's City

THE STALINGRAD BATTLEFIELD TOUR

In 1961 Stalingrad was renamed Volgograd (Volga City) during Soviet Premier Nikita Khruschev's de-Stalinization programme. Volgograd is a major rail junction and can be reached by overnight train from Moscow. Flights from Moscow last one and a half hours or the city can be visited as part of a Volga cruise from Kazan to Rostov-on-Don. The central thoroughfare is Lenin Avenue *(Prospekt Lenina)*, running parallel to the Volga, from which many of the recommended tour locations are easily accessible. Volgograd has rail, river and central bus stations and the airport is a half hour bus ride from the city. There are many hotels of varying quality.

① THE GRAIN ELEVATOR BUILDING

An important strategic point to the south of the city was the massive Grain Silo. This is situated near the railway goods depot south west of the city centre. The present main street runs alongside. It was defended by about 40 soldiers from the 92nd Soviet Marine Rifle Brigade against repeated attacks by elements of 24th Panzer and 94th Infantry Divisions. The Germans managed to reach the building but despite constant shelling and direct tank fire were unable to take control of it. Panzers were kept at bay by determined Red Army men shooting back with armour piercing anti-tank rifles. The heroic statue of a Marine standing outside holds such a weapon. Part of the inscription on the huge concrete cape reads *'Victory in the name of the Motherland'*. The distinctive silhouette of the Silo is every bit as distinctive today on Volgograd's southern skyline as it was in devastated Stalingrad.

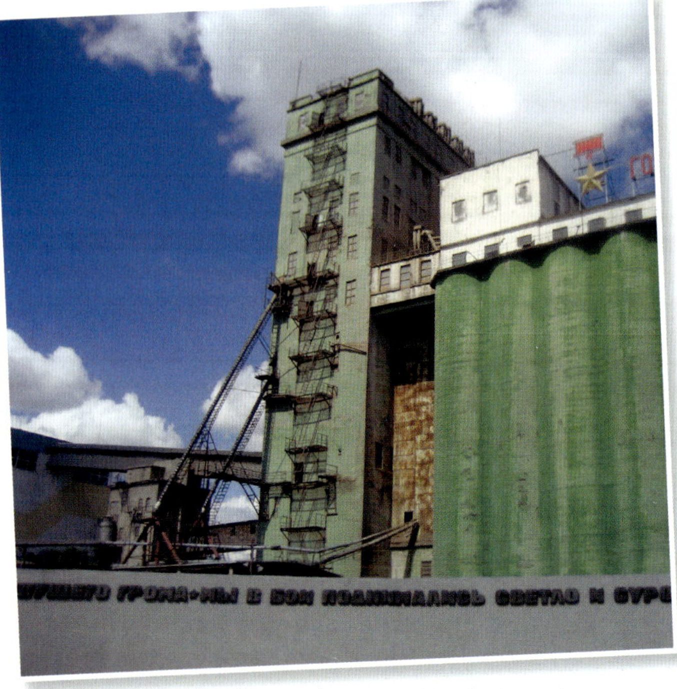

The elevator today, Soviet soldiers fired down from all levels.

Ulitsa Slovetskay
Ulitsa Chuykova
Sheldoeya5 Viceroy
N
0   1 Mile
0   400 Metres
8
7
6
River Volga
Prospekt Lenina
The Railway Station
5
4
3
2
1
BATTLEFIELD STANDS - STALINGRAD 1942/3
STAND 1: THE GRAIN ELEVATOR BUILDING
STAND 2 & 3: FIRE SHIP GASITEL & VOLGA FERRIES
STAND 4: FALLEN HERO'S SQUARE (RED SQUARE) AND UNIVERMAG BUILDING
STAND 5: PAVLOV'S HOUSE AND THE GRUDININ MILL
STAND 6: THE MAMYAV KURGAN HILL, HEIGHT 102 METRES
STAND 7: THE BARRIKADY GUN FACTORY AND LYUDNIKOV'S ISLAND
STAND 8: THE TRACTOR FACTORY.

German Infantryman Willi Hoffman with the 94th Infantry Division wrote in his diary on 16th September 1942:

'Our battalion plus tanks is attacking the elevator, from which smoke is pouring – the grain in it is burning, the Russians seem to have set light to it themselves. Barbarism. The battalion is suffering heavy losses. There are not more than 60 men left in each company. The elevator is occupied not by men but by devils that no flames or bullets can destroy'.

Resistance was not over until the 22nd September, when Hoffman wrote:

'We found about 40 Russians dead in the elevator building. Half of them were wearing naval uniform – sea devils. One prisoner was captured, seriously wounded, who can't speak; or is shamming'.

The Marine statue standing sentinel today grasps a light anti-tank rifle, crucial for the close-in defence of the building.

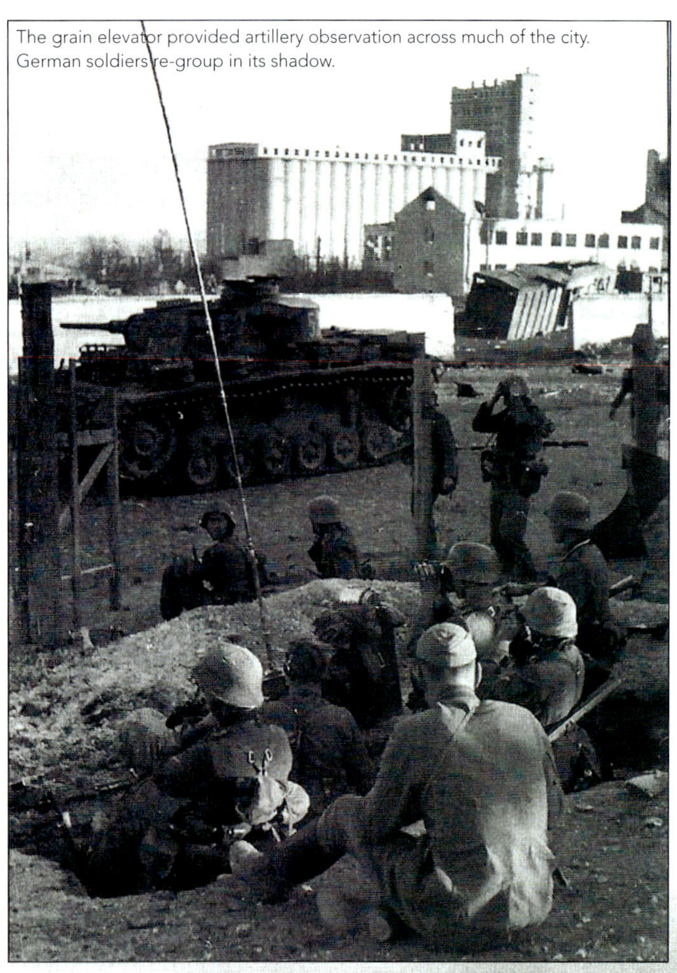

The grain elevator provided artillery observation across much of the city. German soldiers re-group in its shadow.

They captured Andrey Khozuynov from the 92nd Marine Infantry Brigade. He recalled beating off ten attacks alone on the 18th September:

'We economised on ammunition, as it was a long way, and difficult to bring up more.

In the elevator the grain was on fire, the water in the machine guns evaporated, the wounded were thirsty, but there was no water nearby. This was how we defended ourselves twenty-four hours a day for three days. Heat, smoke, thirst – all our lips were cracked. During the day many of us climbed up to the highest points in the elevator and from there fired on the Germans; at night we came down and made a defensive ring round the building'.

Eventually the Germans broke in:

'We sensed and heard the enemy soldier's breath and footsteps, but we could not see them in the smoke. We fired at sound'.[16]

The ghostly silhouette of the elevator building under fire is visible through the smoke of battle across southern Stalingrad.

The fire-ship Gasitel was sunk ferrying troops during the crossings and restored as a commemorative monument after the war.

Ferries on the Volga today, viewed from the Stalingrad/Volgograd bank. The river is a mile wide in places.

②③ FIRE SHIP GASITEL & VOLGA FERRIES

The fire-ship *Gasitel* at the mouth of the River Tsaritsa is situated just south of the main Soviet ferry jetties and is a memorial to the soldiers of the Volga Basin Fleet. These boats ferried 100,000 soldiers across the Volga under fire and took 300,000 civilians back. The *Gasitel* was sunk in October 1942 and brought to the surface after the war and restored; some 3,000 holes were found on the hull and superstructure. Occupying prominent points like the elevator building enabled the Germans to bring down accurately observed artillery fire onto the boats. There is a commemorative breast wall alongside the river where Rodimtsev's 13th Guards Division crossed near the Grudinin Mill. The Russian inscription reads *'The 13th Guards Division stood here and fought to the death. By standing our ground, we conquered death'.* Soviet war correspondent Vasily Grossman captured the atmosphere of the crossings from eye-witness participants:

'Suddenly, a tall and thin bluish-white column of water sprang up about fifty metres from the barge. Immediately after it another column grew and collapsed even closer, and then a third one. Bombs were exploding on the surface of the water and the Volga was covered with lacerated foaming wounds; shells began to hit the sides of the barge. Injured men would cry out softly, as if trying to conceal the fact of being wounded. By then rifle bullets had already started whistling over the water.

'By standing our ground, we conquered death'

'There was one terrible moment when a large calibre shell hit the side of a small ferry. There was a flash of flame, dark smoke enveloped the ferry, an explosion was heard, and immediately afterwards, a drawling scream as if born from this thunder. Thousands of people saw immediately the green helmets of the men swimming among the wreckage of wood rocking on the surface of water.'[17]

16. Hoffman and Khozuynov, *Purnell's History of the Second World War*, Vol 3, P. 1144.
17. Grossman, *A Writer at War*, P. 148.

4 FALLEN HERO'S SQUARE (RED SQUARE) AND UNIVERMAG BUILDING

An Oblisk and eternal flame burns next to the common grave of the city defenders, between Ulitsa Mira and Svietskaya in the centre of Volgograd. There is a poplar tree spectacularly scarred by flame and bullets nearby. This is the only tree in the former Red square known to have survived the fighting, which has since grown to a height of 30 metres. Nearby is the Univermag Department Store building, from which the defeated Sixth Army Commander General Paulus, surrendered in January 1943. The Soviets called the square 'Fallen Fighters' commemorating the Bolshevik dead from the Russian Civil War; the Germans simply called it 'Red Square'.

Right: The scarred poplar tree, the only one to survive the battle in the square.
Below: The oblisk and site of the eternal flame for the City's defenders in Red Square.

unforgettable contribution towards the establishment of a defensive front and the salvation of the Western World'.

The final signal transmitted from the Univermag at 05.45 hours on 31st January 1943 read:

'The Russians stand at the door of our bunker. We are destroying our equipment. This station will no longer transmit.'

British war correspondent Alexander Werth caught sight of a human figure crouching over a cesspool in sub zero temperatures in a yard off this square at the time of the surrender:

'…Noticing us, he was hastily pulling up his pants. And then he slunk away into the door of a basement. But as he passed I caught a glimpse of the wretch's face, with its mixture of suffering and idiot-like incomprehension. For a moment I wished the whole of Germany were there to see it. The man was perhaps already dying. In that basement into which he slunk there was still two hundred Germans – dying of hunger and frostbite. 'We haven't had time to deal with them yet' one of the Russians said. 'They'll be taken away tomorrow, I suppose'.[18]

The Univermag building today, where Field Marshal von Paulus surrendered in January 1943

Inset right: The ruined Univermag building, shortly after its capture in September 1942 displaying the Nazi flag.

Paulus radioed this message to German High Command (OKW) from the building on 24th January 1943:

'Effective command no longer possible. Little change on eastern front; 18,000 wounded without any supplies of dressings or drugs; 44, 76, 100, 305 and 384 Infantry Divisions destroyed. Front torn open a result of strong breakthroughs on three sides. Strong-points and shelter only available in the town itself; further defence senseless. Collapse inevitable. Army requests immediate permission to surrender in order to save lives of remaining troops. Paulus.'

Adolf Hitler responded the same day:

'Surrender is forbidden. Sixth Army will hold their positions to the last man and last round and by their heroic endurance will make an

⑤ PAVLOV'S HOUSE AND THE GRUDININ MILL

Pavlov's House is on the Ulitsa Sovietskaya with the Grudinin Mill nearby on Ulitsa Chuykova (Chuikov Street), next to the Battle of Stalingrad Panoramic Museum. Tank turrets mounted on plinths along the Prospekt Lenina nearby mark the Soviet line of defence as it was on November 18th 1942.

Pavlov's house was originally a four-storey prestigious apartment block commanding a good view across the German positions to the north west and south. It was held by Sergeant Yakov Pavlov with a group of Russian soldiers rarely numbering more than 50 men against repeated German attacks for 58 days. Its protrusion into German territory blocked one of the main enemy avenues of advance to the Volga. The small garrison reported to the large brick grain store, the Grudinin Mill, 300 yards behind. This ruined building has been preserved in its original shell-marked state to commemorate the battle. The mill was an important command post and staging area for troops assembling to reinforce threatened sectors, after crossing the river.

Above, the remains of Pavlov's House today, preserved as a commemorative icon. Right, the original prestigious apartment block, with its floors opened up by artillery fire like the pages of a discarded book.

The Volgograd Battle of Stalingrad Museum with its panoramic painting of the battle forms part of the same complex. Inside is the famous sword presented in 1943 by the British people and King George VI to the citizens of Stalingrad. Zaitsev's sniper rifle is on display as also is the table at which General von Paulus was first interrogated following his surrender.

Pavlov's house was marked as 'a fortress' on German maps. Georgy Potansky with the 13th Guards Division claimed:

'The mill was as strong as a castle. But neither the enemy air force

18. Signals, ed JE Lewis, *How it Happened. World War II*, P. 252. Werth, J Bastable, *Voices from Stalingrad*, P. 277.

'Stalingrad is no longer a town' wrote one panzer officer viewing the destruction shown here of the factory district, 'it is a vast furnace'.

Right: Two views of the ruins of the Grudinin Mill, still preserved in their original shell-pocked state.

nor our own bombed the area around Pavlov's House, the mill and Ninth of January Square because the lines were too close to each other. The only thing that saved us from starving was the fact that there were large quantities of grain in the basement of the mill. We slept on it, and we fed ourselves with it. We often had to grab our guns and grenades and beat off German attacks. Many of our soldiers were put out of commission – some killed, some wounded. The wounded often died because we did not know how to give them first aid, how to bind their wounds. No one had taught us'.

Although the beam end of Pavlov's House was gradually collapsed by artillery fire, the floors hanging down like pages from a discarded book, the narrowness of the approaches prevented the panzers from elevating their guns to engage the upper floors. Pavlov described:

'Our house was assaulted by heavy tanks, we lived under heavy artillery fire. Machine guns were firing without stop. Sometimes we ran out of ammunition. We didn't have enough water and food. We couldn't breathe because of dust and ashes'.

'My God, why have you forsaken us' wrote Leutnant Weiner with the 24th Panzer Division fighting next to the sector:

'Stalingrad is no longer a town. By day it is an enormous cloud of burning, blinding smoke; it is a vast furnace lit by the reflection of flames. And when the night arrives, one of those scorching, howling, bleeding nights, the dogs plunge into the Volga and swim desperately to gain the other bank. The nights of Stalingrad are a terror for them. Animals flee this hell; the hardest storms cannot bear it for long; only men endure'.[19]

6 THE MAMYAV KURGAN HILL, HEIGHT 102 METRES

The Mamyav Kurgan (Hill) is 102 metres high and dominates the city, overlooking the northern and southern sectors and the landing jetties on the Volga River below. It can be reached from the Prospekt Lenina. Some of the bitterest fighting of the Second World War raged across this height, which since 1967 has housed a huge memorial complex commemorating the battle. Dominating the peak is the gigantic 170 feet high statue symbolising Mother Russia, the focal point for the memorial gardens, stone tableaux squares, bas-reliefs and the Hall of Valour all around it. Some 5,500 tons of concrete and 2,400 tons of metal was used in the construction of the majestic figure that stands in place under its own weight. The 95-foot stainless steel sword held aloft has an aperture cut within it to reduce wind resistance.

Above right: The 170-foot high statue of Mother Russia dominates the Mamyav Kurgan.

The view of the present day factory district, still to the north of Volgograd, viewed from the Mamyav Kurgan.

Left: The Germans never quite managed to eject the Soviet soldiers from the east slope of the Mamyav Kurgan.

Two huge concrete water cisterns originally crowned the hill, which was the city's water reservoir. They were transformed into miniature fortresses and became the primary objective for both sides.

A sacrificial insertion by the 13th Guards Division only just prevented its capture, losing 3,000 men in their first battle for the heights. Nikolai Maznitsa fighting with the 95th Division remembered the ominous silences between the German attacks that *'threw themselves in a frenzy at the summit'* on 19th September:

'Then the hill would come alive again like a volcano, and we would crawl out of the shell holes and put our machine guns to work. The barrels of the guns were red-hot and the water boiled inside them. Our men attacked without waiting for orders…

'The slopes of the Kurgan were completely covered in corpses. In some places you had to move two or three bodies aside to lie down. They quickly began to decompose, and the stench was appalling, but you just had to lie down and pay no attention'.

The Germans held onto the western slope, locked in a bloody stalemate that never quite managed to eject the Russians from the east side. Captain Viktor Popov with the 24th Siberian Rifle Division recalled:

'The German attacks were vicious, especially on the right hand side of the Mamayev Kurgan. Here the Germans made use of tanks and self-propelled guns. They knew that from the top they would be able to fire on our gun emplacements over open sights. The Germans attacked without success for a long time, but eventually our battalion on the right flank had to move back, and took up a new position at the foot of the Kurgan'.[20]

The hill was not fought entirely clear until the surrender on 2nd February 1943.

19. Potansky, Bastable, p. 103. Pavlov, B Moynahan, *Forgotten Soldiers*, P. 68. Weiner, Purnell, P. 1148.
20. Maznitsa and Popov, Bastable, Pp. 96-8.

7 THE BARRIKADY GUN FACTORY AND LYUDNIKOV'S ISLAND

'They had two boxes of grenades and they beat the Germans off'

The small 700 metre by 400 metre area just to the south of the Red Barrikady gun factory in the northern factory district is called Lyudnikov's Island. This is to commemorate the epic fight by Colonel Lyudnikov's 138th Infantry Division, which was pressed in from three sides by German attacks with their backs to the Volga, but managed to hold out despite virtual annhilation. These massive attacks into the northern factory district took the pressure off central Stalingrad in November 1942. Ruined blocks dating back to the battle still

Above: Tank turrets erected on plinths, (background) mark the extent of the German advance in November 1942.

Left: German troops pick their way with difficulty through the ruined Red Barrikady factory workshops. 1942.

remain inside the small enclave which remained under German siege until 22nd December. Three tank turrets mounted on plinths show the front line as it was during November 1942.

Soviet correspondent Vasily Grossman interviewed Colonel Gurtiev whose 308th Siberian Division defended the northern part of the Barrikady factory complex. He described the unremitting German attacks:

'On 23rd October, fighting began inside the plant. Workshops were on fire, as well as railways, road, trees, bushes and grass. At the command post Kushnarev and the Chief of Staff Dyatlenko, were sitting in the 'tube' with six sub-machine gunners. They had two boxes of grenades and they beat the Germans off. The Germans had brought tanks to the plant. The workshops changed hands several times. Tanks destroyed them, firing at point-blank range. Aircraft were bombing us day and night. A captured German, a teacher, told us on the 27th about the strict orders to reach the Volga. His hands were black, there was lice in his hair. He began to sob'.[21]

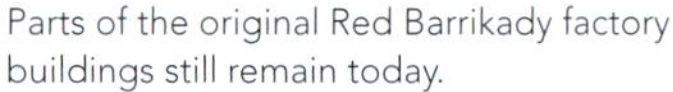

Parts of the original Red Barrikady factory buildings still remain today.

Above: The Soviets held onto the steeply sloping banks of the Volga, just beyond the reach of the Germans.

Left: The Tractor factory gates.

Below: A German infantry platoon pauses to regroup at the edge of the Tractor factory.

8 THE TRACTOR FACTORY.

To the north of Volgograd is the Dzerzhinski Tractor factory. It was the largest factory in the country at the time and had re-tooled to make T-34 tanks. These were churned out even during the battle and were driven off by volunteer worker militias. A T-34 tank has been erected as a monument just outside the factory gates to commemorate the factory worker fighters and their common grave.

'Though tired to the point of exhaustion, we still have the will to force a decision'

The fiercest onslaught began on 14th October 1942 and by the 20th most of the complex was in German hands, with fighting petering out four days later. Temperatures soon plunged to -20°c and still the Russians held a toe-hold to the south of the factory. Leutnant Joachim Stempel was one of only two officers left with Panzergrenadier Regiment 103 attacking towards the Tractor factory, when he recorded in his diary on 27th October:

'We assemble again. Though tired to the point of exhaustion, we still have the will to force a decision. Immediately after breaking cover we suffer dead and wounded in the first few metres! Take cover! Where are the guys that are firing on us? Where is the damned fire coming from? There they are, in front of us. Straight in front of us and behind dark piles of earth, behind the remains of walls the group has taken up positions. 'Go! Flank them on the right and left, we will fire on them from the front'. We attack and take them out…

'How long can this man-to-man fighting, this bloodshed at close quarters, be kept up? I do not know. But it surely cannot last much longer, not with these casualties and losses! But perhaps we'll manage the few hundred metres remaining tomorrow, always tomorrow. The Soviets are holding in the steeply falling slopes to the Volga, and no fire can reach them there. And prisoners have indicated that Russian commanders have their backs there too. They are sitting in their rocky slopes and each evening send new men into battle. We are living in holes in the earth. Stalingrad is nearly completely in our hands. Only the bit in front of us remains…'[22]

21. Gurtiev, Grossman, *A Writer at War*, P. 178.
22. Stempel, J Turner, *Stalingrad Day by Day*, P. 110-11.

It depended whose side you were on - The Hollywood view of Stalingrad

The Battle of Stalingrad.
Vladimir Petrov 1949.

paternal qualities of a coolly confident Stalin. The scenes involving fighting soldiers, such as the legendary Sergeant Pavlov (Leonid Kniazev) are grittier as are the dark turbulent battle scenes. There is one impressive panning shoot, taken from a crane, showing Pavlov's house being fought over, floor by ruined floor.

The film is impressively supported by an epic musical score from Aram Kachachurin, which alternates between the action and stormy poetic moments that characterise the plot. Part 1 with its recreation of the pressing danger enfolding the city is superior to the stilted and thinner second part that deals with the Soviet counter-offensive, showing German strength and morale bleeding to death.

T his black and white film released in two parts in 1949 and 1950 and directed by V Petrov is a heroic Stalinist interpretation of events. Shot in the ruins of Stalingrad, the film portrays spectacular panoramic battle scenes interspersed with slow moving staff meetings that chart the battle's progress. Thousands of Red Army soldiers were employed in the epic action sequences.

Stalin is shown competently handling a crisis, which he is calmly in control of at all times. General Zhukov, politically out of favour during the film's making is conspicuous by his absence. The actors, such as Stalin played by Aleksei Dikiy, Chuikov by Nikolai Simonov and others, bear a striking resemblance to the characters they portray. There is much political Cold War points scoring with the Russians seeking to drive a diplomatic wedge between the more sympathetic Americans and the coldly imperial British, dragging their feet over the launching of a Second Front. Much of the acting is stony-faced propaganda pronouncements, extolling the

Aleksei Dikiy's Stalin looks uncannily like the real figure

Hunde,
Wollt Ihr Ewig Leben?
(Dogs, Do You Want to
Live Forever?)
Frank Wisbar. 1958.

This anti-war film directed by pacifist Frank Wisbar was the West German response to Petrov's Russian film. It was badly received by senior political and military figures in Germany, who found its gritty senseless portrayal of the battle uncomfortable. It was loosely based on the Fritz Wöss novel of the same name and *Last Letters From Stalingrad*. The title is an ironic adaptation of Frederick the Great's criticism of German troops fleeing the battle of Kolin in 1757, when he exclaimed *'You cursed rascals! Do you want to live forever!'*

The film portrays the conflict between a young humane Wehrmacht Lieutenant Wisse played by Joachim Hansen with his authoritarian Nazi commander Major Linkmann (Wolfgang Preiss), both are caught up in the encirclement as tensions soar as their soldiers starve. Wisse is helped by a Russian woman he helped after being captured by the Soviets and gets away but still has to surrender when Paulus orders the capitulation of the pocket.

Linkmann tries to give up but is shot by his own disgruntled men. The film, shot in black and white, is a gritty human drama.

Lieutenant Wisse (right) played by Joachim Hansen regards their bleak predicament from a Stalingrad cellar.

 **Der Arzt von Stalingrad. (The Doctor from Stalingrad.) Geza Redvanyi. 1958.**

The title of this film by Geza Redvanyi is deceptive, being more like a west German version of *Stalagluft 17*. Based on the novel by Heinz Konsalik, it is set in a Soviet POW Camp after the battle. An imprisoned doctor played by OE Hasse is denied surgical tools, but relies on his medical skills to pull his patients through, earning the confidence and respect of his Soviet captors including the female doctor lead.

The film accurately shows German POWs still being incarcerated in Stalinist Russia in the 1950s. German and Soviet antipathy as well as respect is compellingly played in an early film that gets beneath the Cold War skin of the period. It provides a convincingly well-acted portrayal of the human dimension of the battle.

 **Stalingrad. Rudoph Cartier. BBC TV 1964.**

This was a play adapted from the Theodore Plievier novel screened by the BBC in December 1964 as part of an anthology of challenging drama. When it was shown on Hamburg TV the year before, it was condemned as a 'defeatist fabrication' by the General Inspector of the West German Army. He ensured his conscript soldiers were on manoeuvres the night it was transmitted. The play evokes the grim experiences felt by officers and men alike. Generals surrender honourably having sacrificed their men while faceless Nazi officials execute men even in the face of defeat. Common soldiers try to look after each other even as good men are made ruthless by circumstances.

Although clearly produced on a cheap budget, the production is harrowingly convincing, with much of the action conducted in claustrophobic cellars and bunkers. The scenes of panic at Pitomik airfield when the last hospital plane leaves as Russian tanks attack is shot from a Russian tank gunner's slit perspective with abandoned wounded being machine gunned and driven over. The play remains in the BBC archive, and despite being a little dated with some dialogue-heavy scenes, is still an impressively staged and disturbing piece of TV drama.

The film depicts the gradual stripping away of a veneer of humanity by the main players, grouped here at the end. [Bavaria-Perathon]

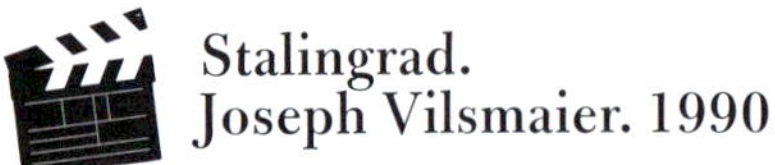
Stalingrad.
Joseph Vilsmaier. 1990.

Stalingrad directed by Joseph Vilsmaier is the second German film to sympathetically portray the battle from the Wehrmacht perspective. It was filmed on location in Finland, Italy and the Czech Republic and follows the plight of a German infantry platoon from leave in Italy after North Africa to Russia, where they detrain to be unwilling participants in the battle for Stalingrad. The tactics and equipment are impressively authentic with the ruined backdrops laboriously reconstructed from colour photographs that have survived the battle.

The fight is seen through the eyes of Lieutenant Hans von Witzland, played by Thomas Kretschmann and two hardened veterans (Jochen Nickel and Dominique Hortwitz) whose fortunes are followed fighting in the factory district and sewers of the city. They are sentenced to a penal unit and face a nightmarish battle with Soviet tanks in the snow on the outskirts of the encircled perimeter.

Having missed the last flight out with the wounded from Pitomik airfield they succumb to the Russian winter. They encapsulate the fate of Sixth Army, tiny figures gradually covered by drifting snow in the film's final haunting scene.

The film delivers a visceral and uncompromising anti-war message convincingly portraying the gradual stripping away of the veneer of humanity from the main players. Some of the scenes, such as those shot with the Russian woman Irina (Dana Vávrová), in the sewer and department store appear hardly credible and are a distraction from the otherwise grim depiction of the epic disintegration of the Sixth Army, although the poignant last shot compensates for this digression.

In 1993 the film won a succession of Bavarian film awards for best cinematography, editing and production. The film is a visual feast, well acted and well worth seeing.

The fight through the factory district is authentically recreated. [Bavaria-Perathon]

The poignant ending of the film (above) is a direct recreation of wartime photographs (below) of the end at Stalingrad.

The Volga river crossing scene with ferries attacked by swarms of Luftwaffe aircraft is spectacular but not authentic. [Paramount]

 ### Enemy at the Gates. Jean-Jacques Annaud. 2001.

This version of the battle directed by Jean-Jacques Annaud portrays the Soviet side, which has been absent from recent versions of the Stalingrad genre. Russian political officer Danilov (Ralph Fiennes) transforms unknown soldier Vassily Zaitsev (Jude Law) into a media hero with his sniper exploits. So effective is Zaitsev that the German army despatches its own master marksman Major König (Ed Harris) to hunt him down.

Apart from a few set piece battle scenes the film does not work well. The disorientated and confusing crossing of the Volga by Russian reinforcements is an attempt to emulate the shock opening of Spielberg's *Saving Private Ryan* but it is not credible. Inaccuracies, with no officers or NCOs to receive the troops on shore, demoralised by Luftwaffe attacks as numerous and compacted as swarms of insects, digresses from the credible reality of the hellish scenes shown. Soviet veterans were so offended by such aspects of the Hollywood-style direction that they insisted that the state Duma should ban it when the film was shown in Russia in 2001. The superfluous love interest with Tania Chernova (Rachel Weisz) detracts from the main plot issue, which is the sniper duel between Zaitsev (Law) and Major König (Harris), applying their total energy and skills to kill each other. This is the only time the film achieves the rare focus and concentration it otherwise lacks.

The film was shot on location in Berlin for the street fighting scenes and near Cottbus in Germany for the Volga crossing, but is unremarkable, despite the $60 million expense. It was partially booed at the Berlin film festival for its simplification of history while glorifying war. Soviet and German veterans were offended by the film, which was in general poorly received. Mixed reviews in the United States lauded the duel but condemned the love story as unnecessary.

There are considerable inaccuracies. The duel was likely pure fiction (and is covered in the Battlefield Detective section).

A fictional Zaitsev (Jude Law) is forced to attack alongside unarmed conscripts who have to retrieve weapons from the dead. [Paramount]

Chuikov the colourful Soviet Stalingrad commander receives no mention and neither does his superior Yeremenko, whereas Nikita Khruschev, the political commissar played by Bob Hoskins, is seen as virtually directing the battle. Ralph Fiennes is unconvincing as the political spin doctor and the tough and ruthless Zaitsev, who had been a Lieutenant in the Soviet Pacific Fleet in the 1930s, is portrayed by Law as rather a callow youth. Ed Harris is more convincing as the German sniper König, a seemingly exhausted and increasingly disillusioned old warhorse.

The film runs out of steam before the end, but is worth a view as a contrast to some other takes of the Stalingrad genre. It offers spectacle as a substitute for the absence of accuracy and emotion.

German master sniper Major Konig (Ed Harris), is despatched to hunt down Zaitsev in the personal sniper duel portrayed in Enemy at the Gates. [Paramount]

BATTLEFIELD EXPERIENCES THROUGH THE AGES

In general, *Battles That Changed the World* seeks to offer a discerning and curious reader an insight into conflicts that had huge impacts on the nations and societies living through their period. The choice of battles in this special publication offers something from the ancient era juxtaposed alongside a middle period and modern military history. Many locations can be exotic, expensive, or complicated to reach, such as Stalingrad on the Volga River, the gateway to Asia. However, you do not have to actually walk the ground to derive the experience - contemporary photographs and maps offer a pseudo battlefield tour, the whole point of this title. Whether you visit or not, there is the immediate benefit of an informative guide with maps and eye-witness accounts to gloss out what can still be seen.

The format concentrates on the human aspect of battle: sight, sound, feel and smell to give the taste of battle as the participants themselves might have experienced it. Three dimensional views of battlefields illustrate what he might have seen from a vantage point.

Commanders are described as their contemporaries would have regarded them. Combatants are examined with an eye for what the average fighter might have seen and heard in the ranks. '*Battlefield Detective*' articles strip off the fictional veneer often left by novelists and filmmakers. It is interesting to review the Hollywood take on historical events and see how often authenticity can be compromised for the commercial or artistic imperative. Joseph E Levine once told his historical advisor on the set of *A Bridge Too Far*, the story of Market Garden and Arnhem, that "he made movies for dollars, not history."

There is no shortage of future topics under consideration, ranging from 'Unlikely Victories' to 'Catastrophic Defeats', 'Invasions' and 'Sieges' and a plethora of like themes. Hopefully, you can join me there.

Robert Kershaw.